OUTL

BIBLE STUDY

G. DALLAS SMITH

GOSPEL ADVOCATE
A TRUSTED NAME SINCE 1855

Gospel Advocate Company
P.O. Box 150
Nashville, Tennessee 37202

PREFACE

Outlines of Bible Study is not a commentary in any sense of the word. It contains but few comments. It is not *"literature"* in the sense in which many object to literature. *It does not study the lessons for you,* but rather guides you in an intelligent study of the Bible itself. It is just what its name implies—*outlines of Bible study*. It simply outlines your Bible study, making it possible for you to study it systematically and profitably.

The questions following each outline direct the student, with but few exceptions, to the Bible itself for his answers. This forces him to "search the Scriptures" diligently to find answers to the questions, and leaves him free to frame his answers in his own language. In the very nature of things, this little book can never take the place of the Bible in class work; for it is absolutely useless and worthless without the Bible, to which it constantly directs the student. *You do not study this little book,* except to familiarize yourself with the plan of study; but you study the Bible itself, this little book serving you only as a *guide* in your study.

The author has spent many hours very pleasantly and profitably in the preparation of this work. He has also taught the courses outlined in the following pages for a number of years with quite a degree of satisfaction. And it is his sincere desire that many others may find both pleasure and profit in the study of the one great Book as herein outlined.

This little book is now sent forth on its mission, which is to lead men to systematically study the one Book, with the earnest prayer that it may accomplish its mission wherever it goes. THE AUTHOR.

other questions which the wide-awake teacher will be sure to ask. In looking up references for answers to questions, the student should not be satisfied to read the verse or verses, or even the chapters indicated, but should read the connections and marginal references and investigate each subject as thoroughly as possible.

With a competent teacher, *who knows his lesson well,* and who is capable of using the drill method effectively, a class may be carried over this course in seventeen days—*one drill each day*—with good results. Of course, in this case, the success will depend largely on the teacher and his ability to impart knowledge by *drilling* the class over and over, again and again, on the principal points.

But, for better results, it is advised that the course be covered in seventeen weeks instead of seventeen days. This gives more time for the students to prepare the lessons, and is more satisfactory in every way. Of course, even in this seventeen-weeks' course, *much depends on the teacher and his fitness for the work.* However, almost any one with some natural talent as a teacher can successfully conduct this seventeen-weeks' course, *if he will faithfully apply himself.*

But where it is desired to go more into details, and to study the lessons more carefully and critically, it is best to give one year's study to the course. For this purpose the questions have been divided into fifty-two lessons, indicated in parentheses. This furnishes a splendid year's work for students of almost any age. Any one with ordinary ability can teach this course successfully, as it gives the teacher plenty of time to familiarize himself with the lessons before coming before the class. This course is recommended for all weekly Bible classes, especially for students above twelve and fourteen years of age.

The author of this little book has taught classes according to each of the plans suggested above, and is frank to say, without appearing to boast, that the results have been, *in each case,* quite gratifying. Of course, the more time that can be given to the course, the better it is. But where a competent teacher can be secured for only seventeen days, he can usually instill new life into a congregation, even in this short time, and lead them to where they can continue the work profitably.

Each student should be provided with some good reference works—a good English dictionary, a Bible dictionary or encyclopedia, a good Bible geography and concordance. For study on Drill I. and Drill XV., "All About the Bible" (price, $1) and "Between the Testaments" (price, 75 cents), by Fleming H. Revell Company, Chicago, will be found very valuable.   THE AUTHOR.

DRILL I.—INTRODUCTION
(Lesson 1—Introduction)

1. What does the word "Bible" mean? It comes from the Greek word "biblos," which means "book," or from the Greek word "biblia," which means "books" or "little books."

2. Why was the name "Bible" applied to the sacred writings? By way of preëminence; it is "the Book of books."

3. When was the name "Bible" first applied to these sacred writings? About the fourth century A.D. (?).

4. Mention some scriptural names that are applied to these writings. Rom. 3: 2; 2 Tim. 3: 16, 17; 4: 1, 2.

5. Define the word "scriptures." The word *literally* means anything written; but "*the Scriptures*" has come to mean *the inspired writings.*

6. Define the word "oracles." The word *literally* means utterances of God.

7. How did God utter these "oracles?" 2 Sam. 23: 2; Acts 1: 16; 2 Pet. 1: 20, 21.

8. About how many men wrote the Bible? Between thirty-six and forty.

9. Why can we not tell just how many? It is not certain as to who wrote some of the books.

10. How many years were they writing, from first to last? About sixteen hundred years.

11. State the number of years covered by their writings. In round numbers, about four thousand.

12. Are there any of these original writings now in existence? No.

13. What do you know about manuscript copies of the Bible? There are said to be some fifteen hundred copies, some containing the whole Bible, and some of them dating as far back as the fourth century.

14. Where are these manuscript copies? The "Vatican" is in the possession of the Roman Catholic Church at Rome; the "Sinaitic" is at St. Petersburg, in the possession of the Greek Catholic Church; the "Alexandrian" is in the Brit-

ish Museum, the property of the Protestants. *Each of these three contains nearly the whole of the Bible.* Then there are many copies in private libraries in different parts of the world.

15. Name twenty Old Testament writers. Search the Scriptures.

16. How many books did Moses write? Moses wrote five books—Genesis to Deuteronomy, *and possibly Job.*

17. What are these five books called? They are called the "Pentateuch," from the Greek word "pentateuchos," which means a fivefold book.

18. Name all the New Testament writers. Search the Scriptures.

19. How many of these were apostles? Search the Scriptures.

20. Tell how many books each New Testament writer wrote. Search the Scriptures.

21. In what language was the Old Testament originally written? Mainly in the Hebrew.

22. In what language was the New Testament originally written? In the Greek language.

23. When and where was the Old Testament first translated into Greek? The work is said to have begun in the year 277 B.C. in Alexandria, Egypt.

24. What is this version of the Old Testament called? It is called the "Septuagint," from the Latin word "septuaginta," which signifies seventy.

25. Why was it called the "Septuagint?" Because it was once thought to have been translated by seventy-two scholars in seventy-two days.

26. By what other name is this version called? It is called the "Alexandrian," because it was translated in Alexandria.

27. Are there any copies of this version now in existence? Yes, and they are said to be the oldest documents in existence.

28. What evidence have we that the Septuagint version is authentic? Scholars generally agree that it is the version from which Jesus so often quoted. If so, it has the approval of the divine Son of God.

29. Into about how many languages has the Bible been translated? About five hundred. *Some say six hundred.*

30. What was England's first Bible? The "Vulgate," a

Latin translation made from the Septuagint version of the Old Testament and the original Greek of the New Testament.

31. What does the word "Vulgate" mean? It comes from the Latin word "vulgata," which signifies "to make common, or public."

32. Who revised this Vulgate version? Jerome, in the fourth century.

33. What do you know about this version of the Vulgate? It is the version that is still used by the Catholic Church.

34. What was the first English translation of note? Wyckliffe's translation from the Vulgate in 1360-1382.

35. How long was Wyckliffe engaged in translating the Bible from the Latin into the English? He is said to have spent twenty-two years on it.

36. How long did it take to make a copy of this Bible with a pen? It required ten months.

(Lesson 2—Introduction—Continued)

1. How did these manuscript copies of the Bible sell? They are said to have sold for about $200 a copy.

2. Who opposed Wyckliffe in his work of translating the Bible into the English language? The Roman Catholic Church opposed him and persecuted him. He was formally tried and excommunicated, and forty years after his death they dug up his body and burned it and scattered his ashes on the River Swift.

3. Who gave us our first printed English Bible? William Tyndale, in 1525, printed the New Testament in English, and in 1536 Miles Coverdale printed the whole Bible in English.

4. What do you know of this first printed New Testament? It is now in the British Museum.

5. What became of William Tyndale? He was mercilessly persecuted by the Roman Catholic Church, and finally, on October 6, 1536, he was strangled and then burned at the stake.

6. What was the first "Authorized Version" of the Bible? In 1537 John Rogers issued a Bible under the title of "Matthew's Bible." Two years later Miles Coverdale and others brought out what was practically a reprint of "Matthew's

Bible" under the title of " Cranmer's Bible." When King Henry VIII. saw it, he said: " In God's name let it go forth among our people." This was the first official authority for circulating the Bible.

7. By what other name was this Bible called? It was called the " Great Bible," because of its size, and also the " Chained Bible," because it was chained to the pulpits of the churches for safe-keeping.

8. What do you know of Henry VIII. later in life? He afterwards ceased to encourage the circulation of the Bible, and in consequence the destruction of Bibles by the Catholics was great.

9. What was the first distinctively Protestant Bible? The " Geneva Bible," which was published by the Reformers in Geneva, whither they had fled during the awful persecution in the reign of Queen Mary, during whose reign some three hundred Bible men were burned at the stake.

10. Why was this Bible called the " Breeches Bible?" Because Gen. 3: 7 was rendered: " They sewed fig tree leaves together and made themselves breeches."

11. What else do you know about this Geneva Bible? It was the first Bible to use *italics* to indicate the words that are not in the original language; also it was the first whole Bible that was divided into verses.

12. What was the " Bishops' Bible?" In 1568 a committee, composed largely of bishops, brought out a version of the Bible, which was called the " Bishops' Bible," because of the number of bishops on this committee. It was never very popular, and soon fell into disuse.

13. When was the King James Bible issued? In 1611.

14. It was the work of how many scholars? Forty-seven.

15. How long were they in translating the Bible? Five years.

16. By what other names is this Bible called? The "Authorized Version," because it was authorized to be read in the Church of England, and the " Common Version," because it is in common use.

17. When was the Revised Version completed? The New Testament in 1881, and the Old Testament in 1885.

18. When was the American Standard Revised Version issued? In 1901.

19. Give a reason why we should have a revision every few hundred years at least. Because the language is constantly undergoing changes. New words are coming into use, and others are becoming obsolete, and still others are changing their meaning.

20. Mention ten important versions of the Bible. See above.

21. Name the two grand divisions of the Bible. The Old Testament and the New Testament.

22. How many books in the Old Testament? Thirty-nine.

23. How many books in the New Testament? Twenty-seven.

24. Name the three divisions of the Old Testament. Luke 24: 44.

25. Name the three divisions of the New Testament. The books of testimony (Matthew to John), the book of conversions (Acts), and the Epistles (Romans to Revelation).

26. Name the three great ages, or dispensations. The Patriarchal Age, the Jewish Age, and the Christian Age.

27. Between what events is the Patriarchal Age? Between the creation and the giving of the law on Mount Sinai.

28. Between what events is the Jewish Age? Between the giving of the law on Mount Sinai and the death of Christ.

29. Between what events is the Christian Age? Between the death of Christ and the second coming of Christ.

30. State the number of years covered by each of these ages. In round numbers, the Patriarchal Age, 2,500 years; the Jewish Age, 1,500 years; the Christian Age, 1,900 years.

31. Mention the religious characteristics of each age. In the Patriarchal Age, family religion; in the Jewish Age, national religion; in the Christian Age, international religion.

32. Mention the most prominent character of each age. Patriarchal, Abraham; Jewish, Moses; Christian, Jesus.

33. When was the Bible divided into chapters? In A.D. 1250, by Cardinal Hugo.

34. When was it divided into verses? In 1551 to 1560.

35. What advantage is this division? One advantage is that it makes possible the use of the concordance.

36. Mention one disadvantage. It frequently severs the connection of parts that are closely related.

B.C. 4004 · B.C. 2348 · B.C. 1921 · B.C. 1706 · B.C. 1491 · B.C. 1451 · B.C. 1400 · B.C. 1095 · B.C. 975 · B.C. 722 · B.C. 587 · B.C. 537 · B.C. 445 (?) · B.C. 4 (?) · A.D. 30 · A.D. 100

Adam	1656 Years	Antediluvian Period
Noah	427 Years	Postdiluvian Period
Abraham	215 Years	Patriarchal Period
Joseph	215 Years	Egyptian Bondage
Moses	40 Years	Wilderness Wanderings
Joshua	51 Years	Conquest of Canaan
Samuel	305 Years	Judges of Israel
David	120 Years	The United Kingdom
Elijah	253 Years	The Divided Kingdom
Josiah	135 Years	Kingdom of Judah (Con.)
Daniel	50 Years	The Babylonian Captivity
Ezra	92 Years	Restoration of the Jews
Judas Maccabeus	400 (?)	Between the Testaments
Jesus	34 Years	The Life of Christ
Paul	70 Years	The Church of God

This diagram may be placed on a blackboard and kept there for reference. It will prove very helpful both to teachers and students

DRILL II.—DIAGRAM OF PERIODS
(Lesson 3—Diagram of Periods)

(For answers to these questions, study the diagram of his-torical periods.)

1. Name the periods of Bible history.
2. What does the word "Antediluvian" mean?
3. How long is this period?
4. Who is the principal character of this period?
5. What does the word "Postdiluvian" mean?
6. How long is this period?
7. Who is the principal character in this period?
8. Define the "Patriarchal Period."
9. How long is this period?
10. Who is the principal character of this period?
11. Define the "Egyptian Bondage" period.
12. How long is this period?
13. Who is the principal character of this period?
14. Define the "Wilderness Wanderings" period.
15. How long is this period?
16. Who is the principal character of this period?
17. Define the "Conquest of Canaan" period.
18. How long is this period?
19. Who is the principal character of this period?
20. Define the "Judges of Israel" period.
21. How long is this period?
22. Who is the principal character of this period?
23. Define the "United Kingdom" period?
24. How long is this period?
25. Who is the principal character of this period?
26. Define the "Divided Kingdom" period.
27. How long is this period?
28. Who is the principal character of this period?
29. Define the "Kingdom of Judah, Continued," period.
30. How long is this period?
31. Who is the principal character of this period?
32. Define the "Babylonian Captivity" period.
33. How long is this period?

34. Who is the principal character of this period?
35. Define the " Restoration of the Jews " period.
36. How long is this period?
37. Who is the principal character of this period?
38. Define the " Between the Testaments " period.
39. How long is this period?
40. Who is the principal character of this period?
41. Define the " Life of Christ " period.
42. How long is this period?
43. Who is the principal character of this period?
44. Define the " Church of God " period.
45. How long is this period?
46. Who is the principal character of this period?

DRILL III.—ANTEDILUVIAN PERIOD
From the Creation to the Flood

Scriptures covered, Gen. 1 to 5.

From B.C. 4004 to B.C. 2348.   Time covered, **1656 years.**

THE CREATION

(*a*) First day—light; day and night.   (*b*) Second day—firmament; water divided, above and below.   (*c*) Third day—land and water divided; vegetation.   (*d*) Fourth day—sun, moon, and stars.   (*e*) Fifth day—animal life; fish and fowl. (*f*) Sixth day—beasts; creeping things; man.   (*g*) Seventh day—the work finished, God rested.   (Gen. 1: 1 to 2: 3.)

THE STORY OF EDEN

(*a*) Location (?).   (*b*) Trees of the garden—"tree of life;" the tree of knowledge; other trees.   (*c*) The temptation and fall—results: (1) Eve doomed to sorrow; (2) Adam doomed to toil; (3) death passed upon all men.   (Gen. 3; Rom. 5: 12; 1 Cor. 15: 21, 22.)

CAIN AND ABEL

(*a*) Their offerings.   (*b*) Abel is murdered.   (*c*) **Cain is** cursed.   (*d*) Seth is born.   (Gen. 4; Heb. 11: 4.)

THE GENEALOGY

(1) Adam; (2) Seth; (3) Enosh; (4) Kenan; (5) Mahalalel; (6) Jared; (7) Enoch; (8) Methuselah; (9) Lamech; (10) Noah.   (Gen. 5.)

THE PROMISED SEED

(*a*) Who is the seed of the woman?   Gen. 3: 15; 22: 18; Gal. 3: 16.   (*b*) Who is the serpent?   Rev. 12: 9; 20: 2. (*c*) How did Christ bruise his head, and how did he bruise Christ's heel?

(Lesson 4—Antediluvian Period)

1. What does the word "Antediluvian" mean? It comes from the Latin words "ante" ("before") and "diluvium" ("the deluge"); hence it means before the deluge, or before the flood.

2. Between what events is this period? See outline.

3. Between what dates is this period? See outline.

4. How many years does this period cover? See outline.

5. How many chapters tell the story of this period? See outline.

6. What was the condition of the earth "in the beginning?" Gen. 1: 2.

7. What book in the New Testament begins, like Genesis, with the words, "In the beginning?" Search the Scriptures.

8. Do we know how long ago since God "in the beginning" created the heavens and the earth? No. "In the beginning" is very indefinite. It could mean six thousand or six million years ago, or a hundred million, for that. So there can be no conflict between science and the Bible here.

9. How did the idea originate that the world is only about six thousand years old? From the fact that it is about six thousand years since God prepared the earth for man and placed him thereon. Gen. 1: 3-28.

10. What was the condition of the earth before God prepared it for man's habitation? Gen. 1: 2.

11. Can we tell how long it had been in this condition? We cannot.

12. What did God do to prepare it for man's habitation? Gen. 1: 3-25.

13. How long was God preparing the earth for man? Gen. 2: 1-3; Ex. 20: 11.

14. How do we figure that it has been about six thousand years since God prepared the earth for man? By adding the ages of the Antediluvian Patriarchs—Adam, Seth, Enosh, Kenan, Mahalalel, Jared, Enoch, Methuselah, Lamech, and Noah—at the birth of their first sons, and adding to this the age of Shem at the flood, we find that it was sixteen hundred and fifty-six years from the creation of Adam to the flood. (Gen. 5: 3-32; 7: 6.) In like manner we can count the time down to about the death of Moses—twenty-five hundred years

2

from the creation of Adam.   This brings us down within the range of secular history.

15. What took place on the first day?   Gen. 1: 3-5.

16. What did God make on the second day?   Gen. 1: 6-8.

17. What was done on the third day?   Gen. 1: 9-13.

18. What was made on the fourth day?   Gen. 1: 14-19.

19. What was made on the fifth day?   Gen. 1: 20-23.

20. What was made on the sixth day?   Gen. 1: 24-31.

21. What did God do on the seventh day?   Gen. 2: 2.

22. Where did God plant a garden?   Gen. 2: 8.

23. Name the four rivers that were associated with Eden? Gen. 2: 10-14.

24. Which two of these have been identified?   The Euphrates and the Hildekel (Tigris).

25. Locate the Euphrates and the Tigris Rivers.   See geography.

26. What kind of trees did God make to grow in the garden of Eden?   Gen. 2: 9.

27. What was the "tree of life?"   Gen. 2: 9.

28. What was the "tree of knowledge?"   Gen. 2: 9.

29. What was the one "forbidden fruit?"   Gen. 2: 16, 17.

30. How were Adam and Eve led to partake of this "forbidden fruit?"   Gen. 3: 1-6.

31. Did the serpent tell the truth or a falsehood in inducing them to eat the "forbidden fruit?"   Gen. 3: 1-7.

32. State some of the results of this sin.   Gen. 3: 14-19.

33. Are we guilty of the "Adamic sin?"   Ezek. 18: 14-20.

34. How did Adam's sin affect all mankind?   Rom. 5: 12.

35. Through whom did we regain all that we lost in Adam?   1 Cor. 15: 20, 21.

36. Who were Cain and Abel?   Gen. 4: 1, 2.

37. Why was Abel's offering accepted and Cain's rejected? Gen. 4: 3-5; Heb. 11: 4.

38. What effect did this have on Cain?   Gen. 4: 5-8.

39. When can we do a thing "by faith?"   Rom. 10: 17.

40. What lesson do we learn from Cain and Abel?   Rom. 15: 4.

41. Who was born to take Abel's place?   Gen. 4: 25.

42. Who was the oldest man of this period?   Gen. 5: 25-27.

43. How is it that Methuselah, being so old, yet died before his father? Gen. 5: 24.

44. Did Enoch go to heaven when "God took him?" Gen. 5: 24; Heb. 11: 5.

45. Give the genealogy from Adam to Noah. Gen. 5 (see outline).

46. Who was the "seed of the woman?" Gen. 3: 15; 22: 18.

47. Who was this serpent that "beguiled" Eve? 2 Cor. 11: 3; Rev. 12: 9; 20: 2.

48. What did John the Baptist say about the "generation of vipers?" Matt. 3: 7.

49. How did Christ bruise Satan's head, and how did he bruise Christ's heel? This probably refers to the great conflict between Christ and Satan, which resulted in Christ's being mercilessly persecuted and finally nailed to the cross (representing the bruising of his heel); but finally rising from the dead, victor over Satan, causing him to lose his power (representing the bruising of his head).

DRILL IV.—POSTDILUVIAN PERIOD
From the Flood to the Call of Abraham
Scriptures covered, Gen. 6 to 11.
From B.C. 2348 to B.C. 1921.   Time covered, 427 years.

THE CAUSE OF THE FLOOD

(a) Predestination (?). (b) Wickedness of the people, caused by the sons of God marrying the daughters of men. (c) Who were the sons of God and the daughters of men? Gen. 6: 1-8

PREPARATION FOR THE FLOOD

(a) Noah's preaching. (b) The building of the ark. (c) Give dimensions and description of the ark. Gen. 6: 9-22; 1 Pet. 3: 20, 21; 2 Pet. 2: 5.

EXTENT AND DURATION OF FLOOD

(a) Rained forty days and forty nights. (b) The highest hills and mountains covered. (c) How long was Noah in the ark? Gen. 7: 11 to 8: 19

AFTER THE FLOOD

(a) The ark rested on the mountains of Ararat. (b) The altar and the offerings. (c) The covenant and its token— the rainbow. Gen. 8: 4 to 9: 17.

THE TOWER OF BABEL

(a) Can you locate the tower of Babel? (b) Why was it built? (c) The confusion of tongues and the beginning of nations. Gen. 11: 1-9.

THE GENEALOGY

(1) Shem; (2) Arpachshad; (3) Shelah; (4) Eber; (5) Peleg; (6) Reu; (7) Serug; (8) Nahor; (9) Terah; (10) Abram.

(Lesson 5—Postdiluvian Period)

1. What does the word "postdiluvian" mean? It comes from two Latin words—"post" ("after") and "diluvium" ("deluge"); hence, after the deluge, or after the flood.

2. Between what events is this period? See outline.

3. Between what dates is this period? See outline.

4. How long is this period? See outline.

5. Give the scriptures that cover this period. See outline.

6. State the cause of the flood. Gen. 6: 1-7.

7. What produced this awful state of wickedness? Gen. 6: 1-7.

8. Who were the "sons of God" and the "daughters of men?" It has been suggested that the "sons of God" were the descendants of Seth, and that the "daughters of men" were the descendants of Cain.

9. What kind of preacher was Noah? 2 Pet. 2: 5.

10. What is it to preach righteousnesss? Ps. 119: 172.

11. Did Noah preach any gospel? Rom. 1: 16, 17; 1 Cor. 15: 1-4.

12. Do you think Peter refers to Noah's preaching in 1 Pet. 3: 18-20?

13. When and how did Christ preach to the "spirits in prison?" 1 Pet. 3: 18-20 (1 Pet. 1: 10, 11).

14. What is said about the gospel having been preached to Abraham? Gal. 3: 8.

15. Was this the same gospel Paul preached? 1 Cor. 15: 1-4.

16. Give the names of Noah's three sons. Gen. 5: 32.

17. Can you figure how long Noah was building the ark? Gen. 6.

18. How did the idea that Noah was one hundred and twenty years building the ark originate? Gen. 6: 3.

19. What kind of material was used in building the ark? Gen. 6: 14.

20. Give the dimensions of the ark. Gen. 6: 15.

21. Give a further description of the ark. Gen. 6: 14-16.

22. How many people went into the ark? Gen. 6: 18; 1 Pet. 3: 20.

23. What else did Noah take into the ark? Gen. 6: 19 to 7: 5.

24. How many of each kind of animals and fowls did Noah take into the ark? Gen. 6: 19 to 7: 5.

25. What were the "clean" and "unclean" animals? Lev. 11: 1-8; Deut. 14: 3-8.

26. What were the "clean" and "unclean" fish? Lev. 11: 9-12; Deut. 14: 9, 10.

27. Classify the "clean" and "unclean" fowls. Lev. 11: 13-25; Deut. 14: 11-20.

28. What reference is made to these "unclean" beasts and birds in the New Testament? Acts 10: 9-14; 11: 5, 6.

29. What lesson was this intended to teach Peter? Acts 10: 27, 28.

30. Is the law regulating the "clean" and "unclean" in force now? 1 Tim. 4: 1-5.

31. Why did Noah take seven pairs of the "clean" animals and fowls into the ark and only two pairs of the "unclean?" Gen. 8: 20.

32. From what two sources did the waters of the flood come? Gen. 7: 11, 12.

33. How long did it rain? Gen. 7: 12.

34. How deep were the waters of the flood? Gen. 7: 19, 20.

35. Where did the ark rest at the end of the flood? Gen. 8: 4.

36. Can you locate the mountains of Ararat? Authorities are not agreed about it. The generally accepted theory is that the ark rested somewhere in the mountainous regions of Armenia, north of Assyria.

37. How did Noah learn that the waters were abating? Gen. 8: 6-12.

38. How long were Noah and his family in the ark? Gen. 7: 11-13; 8: 13-19.

39. What did Noah do on coming out of the ark? Gen. 8: 20.

40. What covenant did God make with Noah at this time? Gen. 8: 21 to 9: 11.

41. What was the sign and token of this covenant? Gen. 9: 12-17.

42. Was Noah granted any privileges relative to food that he did not enjoy before the flood? Gen. 1: 29, 30; 9: 1-7.

43. Where did the descendants of Noah undertake to build a city and a tower?   Gen. 11: 1-4.

44. What other names are given to the land of Shinar? "Babylonia" and "Chaldea."

45. What was the object in building this city and tower? Gen. 11: 1-4.

46. How did God interfere with tne building of this tower? Gen. 11: 5-9.

47. Why was the place called "Babel?"   Gen. 11: 1-9

48. Give the genealogy from Noah to Abraham.   Gen 11: 10-26 (see outline also).

49. Give the genealogy from Adam to Abraham.   Gen. 5 and 11 (see outlines also).

DRILL V.—PATRIARCHAL PERIOD
From Call of Abraham to Egyptian Bondage
Scriptures covered, Gen. 12 to 45.

From B.C. 1921 to B.C. 1706.   Time covered, 215 years.

THE CALL OF ABRAHAM

(*a*) In Ur of Chaldea.   (*b*) Locate Ur.   (*c*) Called of God.   (*d*) Abraham obeyed.   (Gen. 12: 1-4; Acts 7: 1-4; Heb. 11: 8.)

THE JOURNEYS OF ABRAHAM

(*a*) From Ur to Haran.   (*b*) From Haran to Shechem (in Canaan).   (*c*) From Canaan to Egypt.   (*d*) From Egypt back to Canaan.   (Gen. 11: 27 to 12: 20; Heb. 11: 8, 9.)

ABRAHAM AND LOT

(*a*) Lot journeys with Abraham.   (*b*) The separation of Abraham and Lot.   (*c*) Abraham rescues Lot.   (*d*) Meets Melchizedek.   (Gen. 13: 1 to 14: 24; Heb. 7: 1-4.)

ABRAHAM AND ISAAC

(*a*) Isaac the child of promise.   (*b*) The offering of Isaac. (*c*) The trial of Abraham.   (Gen. 17: 15 to 22: 19.)

JACOB AND ESAU

(*a*) The birthright sold.   (*b*) Jacob receives the blessing. (*c*) Jacob becomes " Israel."   (Gen. 25: 19 to 32: 28.)

THE TWELVE PATRIARCHS

(*a*) Name " the twelve patriarchs."   (*b*) Tell about Joseph's dreams.   (*c*) Joseph sold into Egypt.   (*d*) Joseph's experience in Egypt.   (Gen. 37: 1 to 45: 28; Acts 7: 8.)

(Lesson 6—Patriarchal Period)

1. Define the Patriarchal Period. It is that period in which the three great patriarchs (Abraham, Isaac, and Jacob) and the twelve patriarchs (the twelve sons of Jacob—Acts 7: 8) lived.

2. What is the difference between the Patriarchal Age and the Patriarchal Period? The Patriarchal Age includes all the time from the creation to the giving of the law on Mount Sinai—about twenty-five hundred years; while the Patriarchal Period gives us the history of the most prominent patriarchs and covers only two hundred and fifteen years of the twenty-five hundred years.

3. Between what events is this period? See outline.

4. Between what dates is this period? See outline.

5. How long is this period? See outline.

6. What scriptures cover this period? See outline.

7. Where was Abraham living when God called him? Gen. 11: 31.

8. Locate the city of Ur. See map.

9. What was Abraham's name at this time? Gen. 11: 31.

10. What does the word "Abram" mean? "High father."

11. When was his name changed to "Abraham?" Gen. 17: 1-8.

12. What does the word "Abraham" mean? Gen. 17: 5.

13. What was the name of Abram's wife? Gen. 16: 1.

14. To what was her name changed? Gen. 17: 15.

15. To what place did Abraham journey from Ur? Gen. 11: 31.

16. Locate Haran. See map.

17. Is Haran on a direct line from Ur to Canaan? See map.

18. How long did Abraham sojourn in Haran? Gen. 11: 32; 12: 1-5.

19. From Haran where did Abraham go? Gen. 12: 5, 6.

20. Locate Shechem. See map.

21. How old was Abraham when he left Haran? Gen. 12: 4.

22. What promise did God make to Abraham at this time? Gen. 12: 1-3, 7.

23. Who journeyed with Abraham? Gen. 12: 4, 5.

24. Where did Abraham next pitch his tent?   Gen. 12: 8.

25. Locate Bethel and Ai.   See map.

26. In what direction did Abraham journey from Bethel? Gen. 12: 9.

27. Why did Abraham and his company go into Egypt? Gen. 12: 10.

28. Did Abraham practice deception as to who his wife was? Gen. 12: 11-20; 20: 12.

29. On what other occasion did he act in like manner? Gen. 20.

30. On the return from Egypt to Canaan, where did Abraham and Lot go?   Gen. 13: 1-4.

31. Why did Abraham and Lot separate?   Gen. 13: 6-9.

32. What part of the country did Lot choose?   Gen. 13: 10, 11.

33. Where did Abraham then go?   Gen. 13: 18.

34. Locate Hebron.   See map.

35. What promise did God renew to Abraham at this time? Gen. 13: 14-17.

36. In what way did Abraham afterwards befriend Lot? Gen. 14: 1-16.

37. What noted personage did Abraham meet on his return from rescuing Lot?   Gen. 14: 18-20.

38. Who was Melchizedek?   Gen. 14: 18; Heb. 7: 1.

39. What did Abraham do for Melchizedek?   Gen. 14: 20; Heb. 7: 2-7.

40. In what sense was Melchizedek without father or mother—without beginning of days or end of life?   Heb. 7: 1-3.

41. What promise was renewed to Abraham at this time? Gen. 15: 1-5.

42. What did God reveal to Abraham respecting his descendants?   Gen. 15: 12-14.

43. Give the story of Hagar and Ishmael.   Gen. 16 and 21: 8-21.

44. Give an account of the destruction of Sodom and Gomorrah.   Gen. 18 and 19.

(Lesson 7—Patriarchal Period—Continued)

1. What promise did God make to Abraham respecting a child? Gen. 17: 15-19.

2. How old was Abraham when Isaac was born? Gen. 21: 5.

3. How old was Sarah at the birth of Isaac? Gen. 17: 17.

4. What covenant did God establish with Abraham at this time? Gen. 17: 9-14; 21: 1-4.

5. Give an account of the offering of Isaac. Gen. 22.

6. What was the object of this trial? Gen. 22: 12.

7. On what mountain was this trial made? Gen. 22: 2.

8. How old was Sarah at her death? Gen. 23: 1.

9. Where was Sarah buried? Gen. 23: 1-20.

10. Did Abraham have any children besides Isaac and Ishmael? Gen. 25: 1, 2.

11. Relate the story of how Isaac got his wife. Gen. 24.

12. How old was Abraham at his death? Gen. 25: 7.

13. Who buried Abraham, and where? Gen. 25: 9, 10.

14. Who were Jacob and Esau? Gen. 25: 21-26.

15. Give the disposition of the two boys. Gen. 25: 27.

16. Relate the story of the selling of the birthright. Gen. 25: 28-34.

17. What is a birthright? It includes rights and privileges which belonged to the firstborn, such as a double portion of the father's estate and official authority. (See Bible dictionary.)

18. Why did Isaac not go into Egypt during the famine, as Abraham had done? Gen. 26: 1-6.

19. How did Isaac deceive Abimelech, the king? Gen. 26: 7-11.

20. Did God prosper Isaac in this land? Gen. 26: 12-14.

21. Tell how Jacob received Isaac's blessing. Gen. 27: 1-40.

22. What effect did this have on Esau? Gen. 27: 41, 42.

23. Who assisted Jacob in escaping from his brother's wrath? Gen. 27: 42, 43.

24. Tell the story of "Jacob's ladder." Gen. 28: 10-22.

25. What instructions did Isaac and Rebecca give him about marrying? Gen. 27: 46 to 28: 5.

26. Give Jacob's marrying experience. Gen. 29: 1-30.

27. Afterwards how did Jacob get even with Laban, his father-in-law?   Gen. 30: 25-43.

28. Give an account of Jacob's return to Canaan.   Gen. 31: 1 to 32: 21.

29. Under what circumstances was Jacob's name changed to "Israel?"   Gen. 32: 22-28.

30. Give an account of the meeting of Jacob and Esau. Gen. 33: 1-17.

31. How old was Isaac when he died?   Gen. 35: 28, 29.

32. Who buried Isaac, and where?   Gen. 35: 29; 49: 29-33.

33. Name the twelve sons of Jacob.   Gen. 35: 22-26; 1 Chron. 2: 1, 2.

34. Why did Joseph's brothers become jealous of him? Gen. 37: 1-11.

35. Tell of Joseph's being sold into Egypt.   Gen. 37: 12-28.

36. What report did Joseph's brothers make to their father about him?   Gen. 37: 31-33.

37. Why did Reuben not tell his father that Joseph had been sold into Egypt?   Gen. 37: 22-30; 42: 22.

38. What did the Midianites do with Joseph?   Gen. 37: 36.

39. Why was Joseph imprisoned?   Gen. 39: 7-20.

40. How did Joseph fare at the hands of the jailer?   Gen. 39: 21-23.

41. Relate the story of the butler's and the baker's dreams, and Joseph's interpretation.   Gen. 40: 1-22.

42. Relate the circumstances that led to Joseph's liberty. Gen. 41: 1-36.

43. To what important position was Joseph raised?   Gen. 41: 37-45.

DRILL VI.—EGYPTIAN BONDAGE
From Descent into Egypt to Exodus

Scriptures covered, Gen. 42 to Ex. 11.

From B.C. 1706 to B.C. 1491. Time covered, 215 years.

THE DESCENT INTO EGYPT

(*a*) The great famine. (*b*) Jacob's sons go to Egypt to ouy corn. (*c*) Jacob and the whole family go to Egypt. (Gen. 42 to 46; Ex. 1: 5; Acts 7: 14.)

OPPRESSED IN EGYPT

(*a*) Egypt's new king. (*b*) Egyptians jealous of the Israelites. (*c*) Taskmasters set over them. (*d*) Pharaoh's wicked decree. (Ex. 1: 1-22.)

MOSES THE DELIVERER

(*a*) The first three months of his life. (*b*) His famous choice. (*c*) In the land of Midian. (Ex. 2.)

MOSES AND AARON

(*a*) Moses at the burning bush. (*b*) Moses and Aaron sent to Egypt. (*c*) Before the elders of Israel. (*d*) Before King Pharaoh. (Ex. 3 to 6.)

THE TEN PLAGUES

(1) Water turned to blood; (2) frogs; (3) lice; (4) flies; (5) murrain; (6) boils; (7) hail; (8) locusts; (9) darkness; (10) death of all the firstborn. (Ex. 7: 20 to 12: 36.)

(Lesson 8—Egyptian Bondage)

1. Locate Egypt. See map.

2. Between what events is this period? See outline.

3. Between what dates is this period? See outline.

4. How long was this period? See outline.

5. What scriptures cover this period? See outline.

6. Why did Jacob's sons go to Egypt? Gen. 42: 1-3.

7. Which one of the sons was left at home? Gen. 42: 4.

8. Relate briefly their experience on the first trip to Egypt. Gen. 42: 5-34.

9. Relate their experience on the second trip. Gen. 43: 1 to 45: 24.

10. How many Israelites went into Egypt? Gen. 46: 26, 27; Acts 7: 14.

11. In what part of Egypt did the Israelites dwell? Gen. 46: 28 to 47: 27.

12. What do you know about the land of Goshen? Gen. 47: 6.

13. How long did Jacob live in Egypt? Gen. 47: 28.

14. How old was Jacob when he died? Gen. 47: 28.

15. Where was Jacob buried? Gen. 49: 29-33; 50: 12, 13.

16. How old was Joseph when he died? Gen. 50: 26.

17. What oath did he take of the children of Israel before his death? Gen. 50: 24, 25; Heb. 11: 22.

18. When they left Egypt, did they take Joseph's bones? Ex. 13: 19.

19. Where did they bury Joseph's bones? Josh. 24: 32.

20. How were the Egyptians reduced on account of the great famine? Gen. 47: 13-26.

21. Why were the Israelites oppressed in Egypt? Ex. 1: 8-14.

22. Did this oppression have the desired effect? Ex. 1: 8-14.

23. How did Pharaoh next seek to check the rapid growth of Israel? Ex. 1: 15-20.

24. What other means did he employ? Ex. 1: 22.

25. What great character was born about this time? Ex. 2: 1-10.

26. How was Moses saved from the king's wicked decree? Ex. 2: 1-10.

27. Why did Moses leave Egypt and flee to Midian? **Ex.** 2: 11-15; Acts 7: 23-25; Heb. 11: 24-27.

28. How old was Moses when he went into Midian? **Acts** 7: 23-29.

29. Locate the land of Midian. See map.

30. Whose daughter did Moses marry while in Midian? Ex. 2: 16-21; 3: 1.

31. How long did Moses sojourn in Midian? Acts 7: 23-34.

32. How were the children of Israel faring in Egypt all this time? Ex. 2: 23-25.

33. Relate the story of the "burning bush." **Ex. 3: 1-10.**

34. What was the first excuse Moses made? **Ex. 3: 11-22.**

35. What was his next excuse? Ex. 4: 1-9.

36. What was his third excuse? Ex. 4: 10-17.

37. Who did Moses take with him, part of the way at least, back to Egypt? Ex. 4: 20.

38. Relate Moses' experience at the inn by the way. **Ex.** 4: 24-26.

39. Where did Aaron meet Moses? Ex. 4: 27.

40. How did the Israelites receive Moses and Aaron? **Ex.** 4: 29-31.

41. How did Pharaoh receive Moses and Aaron? **Ex. 5:** 1, 2.

42. What command did he give the taskmasters? **Ex. 5:** 4-9.

43. How did this affect the Israelites and Moses? **Ex. 5:** 10-23.

44. How then did God seek to encourage Moses and the Israelites? Ex. 6: 1-8.

45. How did Israel receive this message? Ex. 6: 9.

46. How was Moses a God to Aaron and Pharaoh? **Ex.** 4: 14-16; 7: 1, 2.

47. How was Aaron a prophet to Moses? Ex. 7: 1, 2.

48. How did Moses and Aaron seek to convince Pharaoh, and with what result? Ex. 7: 8-13.

49. How then did God punish him and the Egyptians? Ex. 7: 20 to 11: 10.

50. Name the ten plagues. **Ex. 7: 20 to 11: 10.**

51. Were any of these plagues on the Israelites? Ex. 7: 20 to 11: 10.

52. Why did the Lord harden Pharaoh's heart? Ex. 7: 3-5.

53. How did the Lord harden his heart? Ex. 9: 12, 34.

54. Relate the story of the "potter and the clay." Jer. 18: 1-4.

55. Give God's interpretation of this. Jer. 18: 5-10.

56. Does the story of the "potter and the clay," then, teach fatalism? Jer. 18: 1-10.

57. Then do you not think that Pharaoh was "clay" marred in the hands of the potter (God), and hence had become a "vessel of wrath fitted unto destruction?" Jer. 18: 1-10; Rom. 9: 19-24.

DRILL VII.—WILDERNESS WANDERINGS
From Exodus to Crossing the Jordan
Scriptures covered, Ex. 12 to Deut. 34.

From B.C. 1491 to B.C. 1451. Time covered, 40 years.

CROSSING THE RED SEA

(*a*) Preparation—passover and march to the sea. (*b*) The passage over the sea—pillar of cloud and fire. (*c*) Song of triumph. (Ex. 12: 1 to 15: 21.)

THE MARCH TO MOUNT SINAI

(*a*) At Marah. (*b*) At Elim. (*c*) In the Wilderness of Sin. (*d*) At Rephidim. (Ex. 15: 22 to 18: 27.)

HAPPENINGS AT MOUNT SINAI

(*a*) The law given. (*b*) The golden calf. (*c*) The tabernacle built. (*d*) Nadab and Abihu slain. (*e*) Israel numbered. (Ex. 20: 1-17; Ex. 25: 1 to 40: 38; Lev. 10: 1-9; Num. 1 to 3.)

FROM SINAI TO KADESH

(*a*) Murmuring—the seventy elders chosen. (*b*) Miriam afflicted with leprosy. (*c*) The twelve spies sent. (*d*) The rebellion—result. (Num. 10: 1 to 14: 25.)

FROM KADESH TO MOAB

(*a*) Attempt to enter Canaan. (*b*) Korah, Dathan, et al. (*c*) Aaron's rod budded. (*d*) At Kadesh again—smiting the rock. (*e*) Death of Aaron. (*f*) Fiery serpents. (*g*) Wars. (Num. 14: 26 to 17: 11; Num. 20: 1 to 21: 35.)

IN THE PLAINS OF MOAB

(*a*) Balaam and Balak. (*b*) The plague—twenty-four thousand die. (*c*) Numbering the people again. (*d*) Joshua appointed leader. (*e*) Moses' farewell address. (*f*) The death of Moses. (Num. 22: 1 to 27: 23; Deut. 32 to 34.) (The book of Job should be read here.)

(Lesson 9—Wilderness Wanderings)

1. Between what events is this period? See outline.
2. Between what dates is this period? See outline.
3. How long was this period? See outline.
4. What scriptures cover this period? See outline.
5. What was the tenth plague? Ex. 11.
6. What instruction did God give Israel at this time? Ex. 12: 1-11.
7. What purpose did the blood on the doorposts and the lintel serve? Ex. 12: 13.
8. Why was this called a "passover?" Ex. 12: 13.
9. How long were the Israelites to observe the passover? Ex. 12: 14-17.
10. How was the passover to be observed? Ex. 12: 3-11, 15-20.
11. On what month and what day of the month did the passover begin? Ex. 12: 18.
12. This corresponds to what time of the year according to our calendar? This first month—Abib, or Nisan—corresponds to March-April.
13. What reason did God assign for requiring them to keep the passover? Ex. 12: 14, 26-28.
14. Who were to eat the passover? Ex. 12: 43-49.
15. How often were they to observe the passover? Ex. 13: 10.
16. By what other name is the passover called? Luke 22: 1.
17. Where was the passover first observed after the Israelites left Egypt? Num. 9: 1-6.
18. Where was it first observed after they reached Canaan? Josh. 5: 10.
19. Did the Jews keep the passover in the days of Christ? Luke 2: 41; John 6: 4.
20. Do the Jews of to-day still keep the passover? They do.
21. Why do Christians not keep the passover? No authority for it.
22. Name the two other great annual feasts of the Jews. Deut. 16.

23. Why did God not lead the Israelites on a direct line from Egypt to Canaan?   Ex. 13: 17, 18.

24. How did God lead the Israelites?   Ex. 13: 21, 22; 14: 19.

25. Why did the Israelites murmur at the Red Sea?   Ex. 14: 10-14.

26. How were the waters of the Red Sea divided?   Ex. 14: 21, 22.

27. What was the position of the cloud while they were crossing the sea?   Ex. 14: 19, 20.

28. When did the Lord save Israel from the Egyptians? Ex. 14: 30.

29. When did Israel sing the song of rejoicing?   Ex. 15: 1-18.

30. What reference does Paul make to the crossing of the sea?   1 Cor. 10: 1-3; Heb. 11: 29.

31. Mention three camping places on the march to Mount Sinai.   Ex. 15: 22 to 17: 1.

32. What experience did they have at Marah?   Ex. 15: 23-25.

33. At what place did they find twelve springs and seventy palm trees?   Ex. 15: 27.

34. At what place did God begin to feed Israel with manna and quails?   Ex. 16: 1-20.

35. At what place did Moses smite the rock?   Ex. 17: 1-7.

36. Where and with whom did the Israelites fight their first battle?   Ex. 17: 8.

37. Who distinguished himself in this battle?   Ex. 17: 9-13.

38. Where was Moses during the battle?   Ex. 17: 10-12.

39. Who held Moses' hands up?   Ex. 17: 12.

40. Who visited Moses about this time?   Ex. 18: 1-12.

41. What suggestion did Jethro make to Moses?   Ex. 18: 13-27.

42. When did Israel reach Mount Sinai?   Ex. 19: 1, 2.

43. Locate Mount Sinai.   See map.

44. Under what circumstances did God speak the Ten Commandments?   Ex. 19: 3 to 20: 17.

45. How did God's speaking to the people affect them? Ex. 20: 18-21.

46. What laws did God give to Israel at this time? Ex. 20: 22 to 23: 19.

47. What promise did God make them? Ex. 23: 20-32.

48. How did Israel receive these laws and promises? Ex. 24: 1-8.

49. Why did Moses go up into the mountain? Ex. 24: 12.

50. Did Joshua go with Moses into the mountain? Ex. 24: 13, 14; 32: 15-19.

51. How long did Moses remain in the mountain? Ex. 24: 18.

52. What instructions did God give Moses about building the tabernacle? Ex. 25: 1 to 27: 21.

53. Describe the priest's dress. Ex. 28: 1-43.

54. How were the priests to be consecrated? Ex. 29: 1-37.

55. Describe the regular daily sacrifice. Ex. 29: 38-45.

56. What instructions did God give Moses about the altar of incense? Ex. 30: 1-10.

57. What instructions were given about the lava? Ex. 30: 17-21.

58. What instructions were given regarding the Sabbath? Ex. 31: 12-17.

59. Why did Aaron make the golden calf? Ex. 32: 1-6.

60. How did this affect Jehovah? Ex. 32: 7-10.

61. Then what did Moses do? Ex. 32: 11-14.

62. What did Moses do when he came down from the mountain and found the people worshiping the golden calf? Ex. 32: 15-20.

63. How many Israelites perished at that time? Ex. 32: 25-29.

64. After this, how did God encourage Israel? Ex. 33: 1-23.

65. Why did Moses go into the mountain the second time? Ex. 32: 19; 34: 1, 2.

66. What did God say to Moses about mercy and forgiveness? Ex. 34: 6, 7.

67. What covenant did God make with Israel at that time? Ex. 34: 10-26.

68. How long was Moses in the mountain the second time? Deut. 10: 10.

69. What did Moses do on returning to Israel? Ex. 34: 29 to 35: 19.

70. What do you know about the offerings for the tabernacle? Ex. 35: 20 to 36: 7.

71. Give a brief description of the tabernaclee. Ex. 36: 8 to 40: 38.

72. How many Israelites were encamped at Mount Sinai? Num. 1: 1-46.

73. How long were they encamped at Mount Sinai? Ex. 19: 1, 2; Num. 10: 11-13.

74. Which tribe was not included in this numbering, and why? Num. 1: 47-54.

75. In the place of what did God take the Levites? Num. 3: 11-13.

76. How were the Levites numbered, and how many were there? Num. 3: 14-39.

77. Was the number of the Levites equal to the number of the firstborn among all the tribes? Num. 3: 38-43.

78. What did Jehovah take in exchange for the overplus of the firstborn? Num. 3: 44-51.

79. Between what ages could the Levites serve, and how many were there of this age? Num. 4: 1-49; 8: 23-26.

80. What were the duties of the Levites? Num. 3: 5-37; 18: 1-6.

81. What were the duties of the priests? Heb. 9: 6.

82. What were the duties of the high priest? Lev. 16; Heb. 9: 7.

83. How were the Levites set apart for their special service? Num. 8: 5-22.

84. From what family in this tribe came the priests? Ex. 28: 41; 40: 13-15.

85. Were any of the family of Aaron debarred from serving as priests? Lev. 21: 16-24.

86. What do you know about Nadab and Abihu? Lev. 10: 1, 2.

—P SHOULD NOT LUST AFTER EVIL THINGS.

1 COR. 10:1-5 **(Lesson 10—Wilderness Wanderings—Continued)**

1. What happened to Israel at Taberah? Num. 11: 1-3.

2. Tell about the appointing of seventy elders. Num. 11: 4-17.

3. Give an account of the influx of quails. Num. 11: 18-23.

4. Why was Miriam afflicted with leprosy? Num. 12: 1-15. CRITICISM OF HER BRO./SHE SEEMED TO BE LEADER

5. After this, where did Israel encamp? Num. 12: 16 to 13: 26.

6. Locate Kadesh. See map.

7. How many days' journey from Mount Sinai to Kadesh? Deut. 1: 2.

8. How many spies did Moses send to Canaan? Num. 13: 1-3; Deut. 1: 19-24.

9. What report did the spies bring, and how did it affect Israel? Num. 13: 25 to 14: 10.

10. Who were the two faithful spies, and how were they treated? Num. 14: 6-10.

11. How did the conduct of Israel at this time affect Jehovah? Num. 14: 11-35.

12. What became of the faithless spies? Num. 14: 36, 37.

13. After this, what foolish thing did Israel undertake? Num. 14: 39-45; Deut. 1: 41-46.

14. After this, where did Israel go? Deut. 2: 1.

15. While they were in the wilderness, what is said about one violating the Sabbath law? Num. 15: 32-36.

16. What sin did Korah, Dathan, et al commit? Num. 16: 1-14.

17. What became of Korah, Dathan, and those associated with them? Num. 16: 15-35.

18. What became of the censers of those two hundred and fifty would-be priests? Num. 16: 36-40.

19. What complaint did Israel afterwards make against Moses and Aaron? Num. 16: 41.

20. How did God then punish Israel for this sin? Num. 16: 42-49.

21. Give an account of the budding of Aaron's rod. Num. 17: 1-11.

22. How did God further confine the Aaronic priesthood? Num. 18: 1-7.

23. How were Aaron and his sons rewarded for their service? Num. 18: 8-20.

24. How were the Levites rewarded for their services? Num. 18: 21-32.

25. Give an account of Moses' smiting the rock the second time. Num. 20: 1-11.

26. What sin did Moses and Aaron commit here, and with what result? Num. 20: 7-12.

27. Where did this take place? Num. 20: 1.

28. Who died about this time? Num. 20: 1.

29. How did the Edomites treat the Israelites? Num. 20: 14-21.

30. Where then did Israel go from Kadesh? Num. 20: 22.

31. Who died at Mount Hor, and why did he die at this time? Num. 20: 23-29.

32. Who became high priest on the death of Aaron? Num. 20: 23-29.

33. From Mount Hor where did the people go? Num. 21: 4.

34. Why did God send fiery serpents among the Israelites? Num. 21: 5, 6.

35. What means of healing did God provide, and why? Num. 21: 7-9.

36. Can you name the camping places from here to Pisgah? Num. 21: 10-20.

37. Why did Israel fight with the Amorites, and with what result? Num. 21: 21-32.

38. With whom did Israel fight their next battle, and with what result? Num. 21: 33-35.

39. Where did they next encamp? Num. 22: 1.

40. Tell the story of Balak and Balaam. Num. 22 to 24.

41. Why did twenty-four thousand Israelites die at Shittim? Num. 25: 1-9.

42. Did Balaam have anything to do with this? Num. 31: 13-16.

43. Did Jehovah ever punish Balaam and the Midianites for this sin? Num. 31: 1-20.

44. Did the Israelites increase or decrease during the forty years' wanderings? Num. 1: 1-46; 26: 1-56.

45. Did the Levites increase or decrease? Num. 3: 28; 26: 57-62.

46. How many men were numbered this time who were among the number at Mount Sinai? Num. 26: 65.

47. What tribes were allowed to settle on the east side of the Jordan, and on what condition? Num. 32: 1-42.

48. Why was Moses not allowed to lead the Israelites into Canaan? Deut. 32: 48-52.

49. Where did Moses die, and who buried him? Deut. 34: 1-8.

50. Who became the leader on the death of Moses? Deut. 34: 9-12.

DRILL VIII.—CONQUEST OF CANAAN
From Crossing of Jordan to Time of the Judges
Scriptures covered, Josh. 1 to 24.

From B.C. 1451 to B.C. 1400.   Time covered, 51 years.

CROSSING THE JORDAN

(a) Joshua the new leader.   (b) The two spies sent out.
(c) On the banks of the Jordan.   (d) The march to Gilgal.
(e) Describe the Jordan River and its condition then.   (Josh.
1 to 4.)

ENCAMPMENT AT GILGAL

(a) Locate Gilgal.   (b) Circumcision.   (c) The passover
observed.   (d) The manna ceased.   (Josh. 5: 2-12.)

THE FALL OF JERICHO

(a) Locate and describe Jericho.   (b) Give the order of
march.   (c) How did Jericho fall " by faith?"   (see Heb. 11:
30).   (Josh. 6.)

THE CAPTURE OF AI

(a) Explain the cause of defeat in the first attempt.   (b)
Describe the capture of Ai.   (Josh. 7: 1 to 8: 29.)

THE ALTAR AT EBAL

(a) The law written.   (b) The law read.   (c) "The
mountains of blessings and cursings."   (Deut. 27: 2-14;
Josh. 8: 30-35.)

TWO COMBINED EFFORTS

(a) Five kings are defeated; the sun and moon stand still.
(b) A number of kings are defeated at the waters of Merom.
(Josh. 9: 1 to 11: 23.)

DIVISION OF THE LAND

(a) East of the Jordan.   (b) West of the Jordan.   (c)
Name and locate the "cities of refuge."   (Num. 34: 13 to
35: 28; Deut. 19: 1-13; Josh. 13 to 22.)

(Lesson 11—Conquest of Canaan)

1. Define this period. It is the period during which Israel conquered Canaan, taking possession thereof.

2. Between what events is this period? See outline.

3. Between what dates is this period? See outline.

4. How long was this period? See outline.

5. Give the scriptures that cover this period. See outline.

6. Who was appointed to take the place of Moses? Num. 27: 18-23.

7. How did Jehovah encourage Joshua? Josh. 1: 1-9.

8. What did Joshua then do? Josh. 1: 10, 11.

9. What is said about Reuben, Gad, and the half tribe of Manasseh? Josh. 1: 12-18.

10. How many spies did Joshua send into Canaan? Josh. 2. 1.

11. Relate the experience of these spies in Canaan. Josh. 2: 1-23.

12. On what conditions was Rahab's family to be spared? Josh. 2: 13-21.

13. What report did these spies make to Joshua? Josh. 2: 24.

14. Describe the passage over the Jordan. Josh. 3.

15. What position did the ark occupy while they passed over? Josh. 3: 17.

16. What do you know about the "memorial" stones taken from the Jordan? Josh. 4: 1-11, 20-24.

17. What was the condition of the Jordan at this time? Josh. 3: 15; 4: 18.

18. Where did Israel first "strike camp" in Canaan? Josh. 4: 19.

19. Locate Gilgal. See map.

20. Mention four events of the early encampment at Gilgal. Josh. 5.

21. How did the Lord instruct Joshua to take Jericho? Josh. 6: 1-5.

22. Give the order of march. Josh. 6: 6-9.

23. Give an account of the fall of Jericho. Josh. 6: 15-24.

24. How did the walls of Jericho fall down by faith? Heb. 11: 30.

25. What became of Rahab and her family? Josh. 6: 22-25.

26. What does James say about Rahab? James 2: 25.

27. What curse did Joshua pronounce on the man who should rebuild Jericho? Josh. 6: 26.

28. Who rebuilt Jericho, and with what result? 1 Kings 16: 34.

29. State the cause of the defeat at Ai. Josh. 7: 1-15.

30. Who was found to be the guilty one? Josh. 7: 16-21.

31. How was Achan punished? Josh. 7: 22-26.

32. How was Ai finally taken? Josh. 8: 1-23.

33. What became of the king of Ai? Josh. 8: 24-29.

34. After this, what did Joshua do? Josh. 8: 30-32.

35. Name the mounts of blessings and cursings. Deut. 27: 11-14; Josh. 8: 30-35.

36. Why are they so called? Deut. 27: 11-14.

(Lesson 12—Conquest of Canaan—Continued)

1. Tell the story of the Gibeonites. Josh. 9: 3-27.

2. Who were the Gibeonites? Josh. 11: 19.

3. How did their conduct affect the kings of other cities? Josh. 10: 1-5.

4. In the battle that followed, how did the Lord assist Joshua and the Gibeonites? Josh. 10: 6-14.

5. What became of these five kings? Josh. 10: 16-27.

6. After this, what cities did Joshua take? Josh. 10: 28-43.

7. Where was the next battle, and with whom? Josh. 11: 1-9.

8. Locate the waters of Merom. See map.

9. After this battle, what did Joshua do? Josh. 11: 10-15.

10. After Joshua had conquered the land, what did he do with it? Josh. 11: 23.

11. What part of the land had been conquered by Moses? Josh. 12: 1-6.

12. To what tribes had this been given? Josh. 12: 6; 13: 8.

13. Had all the land been conquered at this time? Josh. 13: 1-6.

14. What was to be done with this unconquered territory? Josh. 13: 6, 7.

15. Why did the Lord not have Joshua complete the conquest? Judg. 2: 20-23. (Ex. 23: 29, 30.)

16. Locate the inheritance of Reuben, Gad, and the half tribe of Manasseh. Josh. 13: 15-32.

17. Where did Caleb get an inheritance, and why? Josh. 14: 6-15.

18. Can you locate the tribes west of the Jordan? Josh. 15 to 19.

19. Who divided the land among the tribes? Josh. 19: 51.

20. What tribes received no land inheritance? Josh. 13: 33.

21. What did they receive for their inheritance? Josh. 14: 4; 21: 1-3.

22. How many cities were assigned to the Levites? Josh. 21: 1-42.

23. What were the " cities of refuge?" Josh. 20: 1-6.

24. Name and locate the " cities of refuge." Josh. 20: 7-9. See map.

25. When did the warriors from Reuben, Gad, and the half tribe of Manasseh return to their possessions? Josh. 22: 1-4.

26. How were they rewarded for their service? Josh. 22: 7, 8.

27. Why did the tribes west of the Jordan threaten to go to war with the two and one-half tribes? Josh. 22: 10-12.

28. How was the matter finally settled? Josh. 22: 13-34.

29. Give the substance of Joshua's farewell address. Josh. 23: 1 to 24: 28.

30. How old was Joshua when he died? Josh. 24: 29.

31. Where was Joshua buried? Josh. 24: 30.

32. How long did Israel serve Jehovah at this time? Josh. 24: 31.

33. When and where were Joseph's bones buried? Josh. 24: 32, 33.

34. After the death of Joshua, who led the army against the enemy? Judg. 1: 1-3.

35. Did Israel ever drive out all the Canaanites? Judg. 1: 27-33.

36. What did Israel do when they grew strong? Judg. 1: 28, 33, 35.

DRILL IX.—JUDGES OF ISRAEL
From Beginning of Judges to the Kingdom

Scriptures covered, Judg. 1 to 1 Sam. 8.

From B.C. 1400 to B.C. 1095.   Time covered, 305 years.

A LIST OF THE JUDGES

1. OTHNIEL. Judg. 3: 7-11. (Delivered Israel from the Mesopotamians.)
2. EHUD. Judg. 3: 12-30. (Delivered Israel from the Moabites.)
3. SHAMGAR. Judg. 3: 31. (Delivered Israel from the Philistines.)
4. DEBORAH. Judg. 4 and 5. (With Barak, routed the Canaanites.)
5. GIDEON. Judg. 6 to 8. (Delivered Israel from the Midianites.)
6. ABIMELECH. Judg. 9. ("The bramble king," who killed his seventy brothers and was killed by a woman.)
7. TOLA. 8. JAIR. Judg. 10: 1-5.
9. JEPHTHAH. Judg. 11: 1 to 12: 7. (Delivered Israel from the Ammonites.)
10. IBZAN. Judg. 12: 8. (Father of thirty sons and thirty daughters.)
11. ELON. 12. ABDON. Judg. 12: 11-15.
13. SAMSON. Judg. 13 to 16. (Great conflict with the Philistines.)
14. ELI. 1 Sam. 1 to 4. (Priest-judge and Samuel's foster father.)
15. SAMUEL. 1 Sam. 7 and 8. (Prophet-judge; the beginning of an unbroken line of prophecies concerning Jesus. Acts 3: 22-24.)

(The book of Ruth should be studied here.)

(Lesson 13—Judges of Israel)

1. Define this period. It is the period during which God ruled Israel by means of judges.

2. Between what events is this period? See outline.

3. Between what dates is it? See outline.

4. How long is this period? See outline.

5. Give the scriptures that cover this period. See outline.

6. How long did Israel obey Jehovah? Judg. 2: 6-10.

7. Why did God allow Israel to be sold into the hands of their enemies? Judg. 2: 11-14.

8. How did Jehovah then seek to benefit them? Judg. 2: 16.

9. Name the judges of Israel. See outline.

10. How did the judges succeed with Israel? Judg. 2: 17-19.

11. Why did Jehovah sell Israel into the hands of the Mesopotamians? Judg. 3: 7, 8.

12. How long did they serve the king of Mesopotamia? Judg. 3: 8.

13. By whom did Jehovah deliver Israel? Judg. 3: 9, 10.

14. How long did Othniel judge Israel? Judg. 3: 11.

15. Who next subjected Israel to servitude? Judg. 3: 12, 13.

16. How long did Israel serve the king of Moab? Judg. 3: 14.

17. Who delivered Israel out of the hands of the Moabites? Judg. 3: 15.

18. Tell how Ehud delivered Israel out of the hands of Eglon. Judg. 3: 15-30.

19. How long after this did Israel have rest? Judg. 3: 30.

20. How did Shamgar kill six hundred Philistines? Judg. 3: 31.

21. Who next oppressed Israel, and how long? Judg. 4: 1-3.

22. What woman delivered Israel, and who assisted her? Judg. 4: 4-10.

23. Who was the captain of the Canaanites, and how was he equipped? Judg. 4: 2, 3, 12, 13.

24. Where was the battle fought, and how did it result? Judg. 4: 14-24.

25. How did Deborah and Barak express their joy on account of this victory? Judg. 5.

26. After this, how long did Israel have rest? Judg. 5: 31.

27. Then who oppressed Israel, and for how long? Judg. 6: 1, 2.

28. How did the Midianites treat Israel? Judg. 6: 3-6.

29. How did Jehovah reprove Israel at this time? Judg. 6: 7-10.

30. Who was called to deliver Israel from the Midianites? Judg. 6: 11-14.

31. What excuse did Gideon make? Judg. 6: 15.

32. How did Jehovah encourage him? Judg. 6: 16-24.

33. What did Gideon do to rid the country of idolatry? Judg. 6: 25-32.

34. Who was associated with Midian at this time? Judg. 6: 33.

35. What further evidence did Jehovah give Gideon? Judg. 6: 36-40.

36. Why was Gideon called "Jerubbaal?" Judg. 7: 1 (6: 28-32).

37. How many soldiers did Gideon assemble? Judg. 7: 3.

38. How and why was Gideon's army reduced? Judg. 7: 1-8.

39. After this, how did Jehovah further encourage Gideon? Judg. 7: 9-15.

40. Tell how Gideon put Midian to flight. Judg 7: 16-25.

41. What tribe became offended because they had no part in this victory? Judg. 8: 1-3.

42. Tell of Gideon's pursuit after the Midianites, and the result. Judg. 8: 4-21.

43. How long did Israel have rest after this? Judg. 8: 28.

44. How many sons had Gideon? Judg. 8: 30.

45. After Gideon's death, what did Israel do? Judg. 8: 33-35.

46. Tell how Abimelech made himself ruler over Israel. Judg. 9: 1-6.

47. Why was he called the "bramble king?" Judg. 9: 7-15.

48. Give the substance of Jotham's address to the people of Shechem. Judg. 9: 7-21.

49. How were the men of Shechem punished for making Abimelech king? Judg. 9: 23-49.

50. How did Abimelech meet his death? Judg. 9: 50-55.

51. Why was Shechem destroyed and Abimelech killed? Judg. 9: 56, 57.

52. How long did Tola judge Israel? Judg. 10: 1, 2.

53. How long did Jair judge Israel? Judg. 10: 3.

(Lesson 14—Judges of Israel—Continued)

1. After this, how did Israel sin against Jehovah? Judg. 10: 6.

2. Into whose hands did Jehovah sell them? Judg. 10: 7.

3. How long were they oppressed at this time? Judg. 10: 8, 9.

4. How did Jehovah reprove them when they cried unto him? Judg. 10: 10-14.

5. What did Israel then do? Judg. 10: 15, 16.

6. Who next made war against Israel? Judg. 11: 4.

7. Who was selected to lead Israel against the Ammonites? Judg. 11: 5, 6.

8. How had Jephthah been treated by his brethren? Judg. 11: 1-3, 7.

9. What promise did they make Jephthah? Judg. 11: 8-11.

10. Why did the Ammonites say they were come up against Israel? Judg. 11: 12, 13.

11. How did Jephthah answer this? Judg. 11: 14-27.

12. What rash vow did Jephthah make on going to battle with Ammon? Judg. 11: 29-31.

13. Give the results of the battle. Judg. 11: 32, 33.

14. Who met Jephthah on his return? Judg. 11: 34.

15. How did this affect Jephthah? Judg. 11: 35.

16. How did Jephthah's daughter encourage her father, and what request did she make? Judg. 11: 36-38.

17. Did Jephthah sacrifice his daughter? Judg. 11: 39.

18. What custom originated here? Judg. 11: 39, 40.

19. What tribe was offended because they had no part in Jephthah's victory? Judg. 12: 1.

20. How were they punished for this? Judg. 12: 2-6.

21. Relate the story of the word "Shibboleth." Judg. 12: 5, 6.

22. How long did Jephthah judge Israel? Judg. 12: 7.

23. Who next judged Israel, and how long? Judg. 12: 8-10.

24. After this, who judged Israel, and how long? Judg. 12: 11, 12.

25. Who next judged Israel, and how long? Judg. 12: 13-15.

26. After this, who oppressed Israel, and how long? Judg. 13: 1.

27. What extraordinary character was born and reared during these years? Judg. 13: 2-25.

28. How did Samson become connected with the Philistines? Judg. 14: 1-14.

29. Relate "Samson's riddle." Judg. 14: 14.

30. How was the riddle made known to the Philistines, and what did it mean? Judg. 14: 15-18.

31. Where did Samson get the thirty garments to redeem his promise? Judg. 14: 19.

32. Why and how did Samson destroy the Philistines' corn fields? Judg. 15: 1-6.

33. Why and how did Samson kill one thousand Philistines? Judg. 15: 6-16.

34. How long did Samson judge Israel? Judg. 15: 20; 16: 31.

35. Tell the story of Samson and Delilah. Judg. 16: 4-22.

36. How did Samson finally avenge himself? Judg. 16: 23-31.

37. After this, when Israel had no judge, how did they conduct themselves? Judg. 17: 6 to 21: 25.

38. How long did Eli judge Israel? 1 Sam. 4: 18.

39. What other office did Eli hold? 1 Sam. 1: 9.

40. What do you know about Eli's sons? 1 Sam. 2: 12-25.

41. How did Eli die? 1 Sam. 4: 1-18.

42. How old was Eli at his death? 1 Sam. 4: 15.

43. How long did the Philistines keep the ark? 1 Sam. 6: 1.

44. Why did they not keep it longer? 1 Sam. 5.

45. Where did they send it? 1 Sam. 6: 10-16.

46. How many men of Beth-shemesh were smitten, and why? 1 Sam. 6: 19.

47. Where was the ark taken next? 1 Sam. 7: 1.

48. How long did the ark remain in Abinadab's house? 1 Sam. 7: 2; 2 Sam. 6: 1-4; 1 Chron. 13: 5-7.

49. What vow did Hannah make respecting Samuel before his birth? 1 Sam. 1: 9-11.

50. Where and how was Samuel trained for the service of Jehovah? 1 Sam. 1: 24-28; 2: 18, 19; 3: 1.

51. Relate the story of Samuel's vision and call. 1 Sam. 3: 1-14.

52. Who finally delivered Israel from the Philistines? 1 Sam. 7: 3-11.

53. Give the origin of the word "Eben-ezer." 1 Sam. 7: 12.

54. Where and how long did Samuel judge Israel? 1 Sam. 7: 15-17.

55. Relate the story of Ruth. Ruth 1 to 4.

56. Why should the story of Ruth be studied here? Ruth 1: 1.

DRILL X.—UNITED KINGDOM
From Origin of the Kingdom to the Division

Scriptures covered, 1 Sam. 9 to 1 Kings 11; 1 Chron. 10 to 2 Chron. 9.

From B.C. 1095 to B.C. 975. Time covered, 120 years.

THE CALL FOR A KING

(*a*) Cause? (1) Samuel's sons did evil; (2) the desire to be like others. (*b*) Samuel's bitter grief. (*c*) God's rule rejected. (1 Sam. 8.)

THE REIGN OF SAUL

(*a*) His anointing by Samuel. (*b*) His great battles. (*c*) His great sin. (*d*) He is rejected. (1 Sam. 9: 1 to 31: 13.)

THE REIGN OF DAVID

The Genealogy.—(1) Isaac. (2) Jacob. (3) Judah. (4) Phares. (5) Esrom. (6) Aram. (7) Aminadab. (8) Naasson. (9) Salmon. (10) Boaz. (11) Obed. (12) Jesse. (13) David—(a) His rise to prominence. (*b*) His anointings. (*c*) The new tabernacle built at Jerusalem. (*d*) Collection of material for the temple. (*e*) His great sin. (2 Sam. 1: 1 to 1 Kings 2: 12.)

THE REIGN OF SOLOMON

(*a*) Solomon's wise choice. (*b*) The temple built. (*c*) "Solomon's glory." (*d*) His writings. (*e*) His apostasy—state the cause. (1 Kings 2: 13 to 11: 43.)

THE RISE OF THE PROPHETS

(*a*) Samuel. (*b*) David. (*c*) Gad. (*d*) Nathan. (*e*) Ahijah. (*f*) Iddo.

(Psalms, Proverbs, Song of Solomon, and Ecclesiastes should be studied here.)

(Lesson 15—United Kingdom)

1. Define this period. It is the period during which all the twelve tribes were, in the main, united under one king at the time.

2. Between what events is this period? See outline.

3. Between what dates is this period? See outline.

4. How long is this period? See outline.

5. What scriptures cover this period? See outline.

6. What reason, or excuse, did Israel give for asking for a king? 1 Sam. 8: 1-5.

7. How did this request affect Samuel, and what did he do? 1 Sam. 8: 6.

8. What did the Lord tell Samuel? 1 Sam. 8: 7-9.

9. What did Samuel do, and what was the result? 1 Sam. 8: 10-22.

10. Who was the first king over Israel, and who anointed him? 1 Sam. 9: 1 to 10: 1.

11. Under what circumstances was Saul led to Samuel? 1 Sam. 9.

12. After this, how did God prepare Saul for this office? 1 Sam. 10: 10, 11.

13. When and where was Saul publicly proclaimed king? 1 Sam. 10: 17-23.

14. Tell of Saul's victory over the Ammonites. 1 Sam. 11: 1-11.

15. After this, how and where was Saul further confirmed in his office as king? 1 Sam. 11: 14, 15.

16. Give the substance of Samuel's speech to Israel. 1 Sam. 12: 1-25.

17. How old was Saul when he began to reign? 1 Sam. 13: 1.

18. What sin did he commit at Gilgal? 1 Sam. 13: 5-15.

19. Why did Israel have no swords at this time? 1 Sam. 13: 19-23.

20. Describe the victory of Beth-aven. 1 Sam. 14: 16-23.

21. Relate the story of Jonathan's eating the honey. 1 Sam. 14: 24-46.

22. Against whom did Saul at this time wage war, and with what result? 1 Sam. 14: 47, 48.

23. After this, what great sin did Saul commit? 1 Sam. 15: 1-35.

24. Then what did Jehovah tell Samuel to do? 1 Sam. 16: 1-5.

25. Give an account of David's anointing. 1 Sam. 16: 7-13.

26. Under what circumstances was David brought into Saul's house? 1 Sam. 16: 14-23.

(Lesson 16—United Kingdom—Continued)

1. Tell the story of David and Goliath. 1 Sam. 17.

2. Who became David's lifelong friend at this time? 1 Sam. 18: 1-5.

3. What first led Saul to become jealous of David? 1 Sam. 18: 6-9.

4. State the different ways in which Saul sought David's life. 1 Sam. 18 and 19.

5. Give the substance of the covenant between David and Jonathan. 1 Sam. 20: 1-16.

6. Relate the story of the "three arrows." 1 Sam. 20: 17-42.

7. Tell of David's eating the showbread. 1 Sam. 21: 1-6.

8. What weapon did David receive at Nob? 1 Sam. 21: 7-9.

9. Tell about David in the city of Gath. 1 Sam. 21: 10-15.

10. What do you know about David and the cave of Adullam? 1 Sam. 22: 1, 2.

11. How did David provide for his parents? 1 Sam. 22: 3, 4.

12. Give an account of the slaughter of the priests. 1 Sam. 22: 6-19.

13. Tell of David's experience at Keilah. 1 Sam. 23: 1-14.

14. Give an account of Jonathan's visit to David. 1 Sam. 23: 15-18.

15. After this, who proposed to deliver David into Saul's hands, and with what result? 1 Sam. 23: 19-29.

16. Under what circumstances did David cut off Saul's garment? 1 Sam. 24: 1-22.

17. Who died about this time? 1 Sam. 25: 1.

18. Relate the story of Nabal. 1 Sam. 25: 2-42.

19. Give an account of David's taking Saul's sword. 1 Sam. 26.

20. After this, where did David go, and how long did he sojourn there? 1 Sam. 27: 1-7.

21. How many men of war were with David at this time? 1 Sam. 27: 2.

22. Relate the story of Saul's visit to the witch of Endor. 1 Sam. 28.

23. Why were David and his men not allowed to fight with the Philistines against Saul? 1 Sam. 29.

24. Give David's experiences at Ziklag. 1 Sam. 30.

25. How long had Saul reigned? Acts 13: 21.

26. Give an account of the battle between the Philistines and the Israelites and of Saul's death. 1 Sam. 31.

27. How did David learn of the death of Saul, and how did it affect him? 2 Sam. 1.

(Lesson 17—United Kingdom—Continued)

1. When, where, and by whom was David anointed king the second time? 2 Sam. 2: 1-4.

2. How long did David reign in Hebron over Judah alone? 2 Sam. 2: 11.

3. Who was king over the other tribes at this time? 2 Sam. 2: 8-11.

4. Tell of the battle of Gibeon. 2 Sam. 2: 12-32.

5. What do you know about war between the house of Saul and the house of David? 2 Sam. 3: 1.

6. How were the other tribes of Israel finally brought over to David? 2 Sam. 3: 6-21.

7. Give an account of Abner's death. 2 Sam. 3: 22-29.

8. Tell of the death of Ishbosheth. 2 Sam. 4: 1-12.

9. Where and by whom was David anointed the third time? 2 Sam. 5: 1-13.

10. To what city did David remove after this? 2 Sam. 5: 6-10; 1 Chron. 11: 4-9.

11. Give an account of the bringing of the ark to Jerusalem. 2 Sam. 6.

12. Why was David forbidden to build the temple? 2 Sam. 7: 1-17; 1 Chron. 17: 1-15; 22: 7, 8.

13. What was David allowed to do? 1 Chron. 22: 2-14; 28: 11-19; 29: 1-9; 2 Chron. 3: 1.

14. How did David treat Jonathan's son? 2 Sam. 9.

15. Tell of the combined effort of the Syrians and Ammonites to fight against Israel. 2 Sam. 10.

16. What great sin did David commit? 2 Sam. 11.

17. Give the origin of the expression, " Thou art the man." 2 Sam. 12: 1-7.

18. How was David punished for his sin? 2 Sam. 12: 10-23.

19. Tell how Absalom "stole the hearts of the men of Israel." 2 Sam. 15: 1-6.

20. Tell of Absalom's conspiracy and death. 2 Sam. 15: 7-18; 18: 1-14.

21. How did David receive the news of Absalom's death? 2 Sam. 18: 19-33.

22. After this, who rebelled against David? 2 Sam. 20: 1-22.

23. State the cause of the three years' famine and how it was ended. 2 Sam. 21: 1-14.

24. Give an account of David's numbering Israel and the result. 2 Sam. 24.

25. When David was old, who sought to make himself king? 1 Kings 1: 1-10.

26. How were Adonijah's plans all broken up? 1 Kings 1: 11-53.

27. Give the substance of David's charge to Solomon. 1 Kings 2: 1-9.

28. How long did David reign, and where was he buried? 2 Sam. 5: 5; 1 Kings 2: 10, 11.

(Lesson 18—United Kingdom—Continued)

1. Tell of the death of Adonijah, Abiathar, and Joab. 1 Kings 2: 13-34.

2. Tell of Solomon's wise choice. 1 Kings 3: 4-15.

3. What is said of Solomon's wisdom? 1 Kings 4: 29-31, 34.

4. How did Solomon, on one occasion, display his wisdom?
1 Kings 3: 16-28.

5. Tell of Solomon's provisions for one day. 1 Kings 4:
22, 23.

6. How many songs and proverbs did Solomon write? 1
Kings 4: 32.

7. Who furnished Solomon material for building the temple? 1 Kings 5: 1-10; 2 Chron. 2.

8. How did Solomon reward Hiram for his services? 1
Kings 5: 11; 9: 10, 11.

9. How many men did Solomon use in preparing material
for the temple? 1 Kings 5: 13-18.

10. Who were these men? 1 Kings 9: 15-23; 2 Chron.
2: 17, 18.

11. How was the timber brought from Lebanon to Jerusalem? 1 Kings 5: 9; 2 Chron. 2: 16.

12. When did Solomon begin work on the temple? 1
Kings 6: 1.

13. How long was the temple in building? 1 Kings 6:
37, 38.

14. Give the dimensions and description of the temple. 1
Kings 6: 2-36; 2 Chron. 3; 2 Chron. 4: 22.

15. Who wrought the work in brass for Solomon? 1 Kings
7: 13-47.

16. Describe the molten sea. 1 Kings 7: 23-26.

17. What furnishings for the temple were made of gold?
1 Kings 7: 48-50; 2 Chron. 4: 19-22.

18. Then what was brought into the temple? 1 Kings 7:
51 to 8: 11; 2 Chron. 5: 1-9.

19. What was in the ark at this time? 1 Kings 8: 9; 2
Chron. 5: 10.

20. Give the substance of Solomon's address to Israel. 1
Kings 8: 12-21; 2 Chron. 6: 1-11.

21. Give the substance of Solomon's prayer at the dedication of the temple. 1 Kings 8: 22-61; 2 Chron. 6: 12-42.

22. What do you know about the feast of dedication? 1
Kings 8: 62-66; 2 Chron. 7: 4-10.

23. Did the Lord hear Solomon's prayer? 1 Kings 9: 1-3; 2 Chron. 7: 12-15.

24. What did the Lord say about Solomon's family and the temple? 1 Kings 9: 4-9; 2 Chron. 7: 17-22.

25. Give an account of the visit of the Queen of Sheba to Solomon. 1 Kings 10: 1-13; 2 Chron. 9: 1-12.

26. Tell of Solomon's wealth and glory. 1 Kings 10; 2 Chron. 9: 13-28; 1: 14-17.

27. Who led Solomon astray in his old days? 1 Kings 11: 1-3.

28. How many wives had Solomon? 1 Kings 11: 3.

29. In what way did these women lead Solomon to sin? 1 Kings 11: 4-8.

30. To what did this sin lead Solomon? 1 Kings 11: 9-13.

31. Give an account of Ahijah's prophecy. 1 Kings 11: 26-40.

32. How long did Solomon reign? 1 Kings 11: 41-43; 2 Chron. 9: 30.

33. What does the word "Solomon" mean? See Bible dictionary. (1 Chron. 22: 9.)

34. Were there any wars with the nations during the reign of Solomon? 1 Kings 4: 24; 5: 12; 1 Chron. 22: 9.

DRILL XI.—DIVIDED KINGDOM
From Division of Kingdom to Fall of Israel

Scriptures covered, 1 Kings 12 to 2 Kings 20; 2 Chron. 10 to 32.

From B.C. 975 to B.C. 722. Time covered, 253 years.

CAUSE OF THE DIVISION

(a) Rejecting God's order (?). (b) Rehoboam's stubbornness. (c) Was it predestinated? (1 Sam. 8; 1 Kings 12.)

THE CAPITALS

(a) The capital of Judah remained at Jerusalem. (b) The capital of Israel was first at Shechem, then at Tirzah, and finally removed to Samaria. (1 Kings 12: 25; 16: 21-28.)

A LIST OF THE KINGS

(a) *Judah*	(b) *Israel*
1. Rehoboam (17 years).	1. Jeroboam (22 years).
2. Abijah (3 years).	2. Nadab (2 years)
	3. Baasha (24 years).
3. Asa (41 years).	4. Elah (2 years).
4. Jehoshaphat (25 years).	5. Zimri (7 days).
	6. Omri (12 years).
5. Jehoram (8 years).	7. Ahab (12 years).
6. Ahaziah (1 year).	8. Ahaziah (2 years).
	9. Jehoram (12 years).
7. Athaliah (6 years).	10. Jehu (28 years).
8. Joash (40 years)	11. Jehoahaz (17 years).
	12. Jehoash (16 years).
9. Amaziah (29 years).	13. Jeroboam II. (41 years).
10. Uzziah (52 years).	14. Zachariah (6 months).
	15. Shallum (1 month).
11. Jotham (16 years).	16. Menahem (10 years).
12. Ahaz (16 years).	17. Pekahiah (2 years).
	18. Pekah (20 years).
13. Hezekiah (29 years).	19. Hoshea (9 years).

(Isaiah, Hoshea, Amos, Micah, Jonah, and Joel should be studied here.)

(Lesson 19—Divided Kingdom)

1. Between what events is this period? See outline.
2. Between what dates is this period? See outline.
3. How long is this period? See outline.
4. What scriptures cover this period? See outline.
5. Give an account of how the division was brought about. 1 Kings 12: 1-20; 2 Chron. 10.
6. Who had foretold this division? 1 Kings 11: 26-39.
7. How many tribes rebelled? 1 Kings 12: 20; 2 Chron. 11: 5-12.
8. Name the kings of Judah. See outline.
9. How long did Rehoboam reign? 1 Kings 14: 21.
10. How did Israel sin during the reign of Rehoboam? 1 Kings 14: 21-24.
11. What do you know about Abijam and his reign? 1 Kings 15: 1-6; 2 Chron. 13.
12. What do you know about Asa and his reign? 1 Kings 15: 9-24; 2 Chron. 14 to 16.
13. Give an account of Jehoshaphat's reign. 1 Kings 22: 41-50; 2 Chron. 17.
14. Why did Jehu, the prophet, reprove Jehoshaphat? 2 Chron. 19: 1, 2.
15. Give an account of Jehoshaphat's victory over Moab and Ammon. 2 Chron. 20: 1-30.
16. Give an account of Jehoram's reign. 2 Kings 8: 16-19; 2 Chron. 21.
17. What do you know about Ahaziah and his reign? 2 Kings 8: 25-29; 2 Chron. 22: 1-9.
18. Give an account of Athaliah's usurpation. 2 Kings 11: 1-3; 2 Chron. 22: 10-12.
19. Give an account of Athaliah's death. 2 Kings 11: 4-16; 2 Chron. 23: 1-15.
20. How old was Joash when he began to reign, and how long did he reign? 2 Kings 12: 1.
21. Who was Joash, and how had his life been saved? 2 Kings 11: 1-3; 2 Chron. 22: 10-12.
22. Give an account of Joash's repairing the temple. 2 Kings 12: 4-17; 2 Chron. 24: 4-14.
23. After the death of Jehoida, what did Joash do? 2 Chron. 24: 15-22.

24. How did Joash meet his death? 2 Kings 12: 19-21; 2 Chron. 24: 25-27.

25. Who avenged the death of Joash, and how? 2 Kings 14: 1-7; 2 Chron. 25: 3, 4.

26. After this, what sin did Amaziah fall into? 2 Chron. 25: 14-16.

27. Give an account of Amaziah's victory over the Edomites. 2 Chron. 25: 5-13.

28. How did Amaziah provoke the king of Israel, and with what results? 2 Kings 14: 8-14; 2 Chron. 25: 17-24.

29. What do you know about Amaziah and his reign further? 2 Kings 14: 1-4; 2 Chron. 25: 1, 2.

30. How did Amaziah meet his death? 2 Kings 14: 17-20; 2 Chron. 25: 25-28.

31. Give an account of the reign of Azariah, or Uzziah. 2 Kings 15: 1-7; 2 Chron. 26: 1-15.

32. Why was Uzziah smitten with leprosy? 2 Chron. 26: 16-23.

33. Who reigned in Uzziah's stead? 2 Kings 15: 7; 2 Chron. 26: 23.

34. What do you know about Jotham's reign? 2 Kings 15: 32-38; 2 Chron. 27.

35. Tell what you know about Ahaz's reign. 2 Kings 16; 2 Chron. 28.

36. Give an account of Hezekiah's reign. 2 Kings 16: 20; 2 Chron. 29.

37. Give an account of the great passover kept by Hezekiah. 2 Chron. 30.

38. Tell about Hezekiah's reforms. 2 Chron. 31.

39. Who besieged Jerusalem in Hezekiah's time, and with what result? 2 Chron. 32: 1-23.

40. Tell about Hezekiah's sickness. 2 Kings 20: 1-7; 2 Chron. 32: 24-26.

41. What prophet visited Hezekiah, and what prophecy did he utter? 2 Kings 20: 16-21.

(Lesson 20—Divided Kingdom—Continued)

1. Name the kings of Israel. See outline.

2. What position had Jeroboam held with Solomon? 1 Kings 11: 26-28.

3. Who had foretold that he should become king? 1 Kings 11: 29-38.

4. What did Jeroboam do to prevent Israel returning to the house of David? 1 Kings 12: 25-33.

5. Who came out of Judah to prophesy against Jeroboam's altar? 1 Kings 13: 1.

6. What became of this "man of God?" 1 Kings 13: 1-32.

7. Give an account of the visit of Jeroboam's wife to the prophet Abijah at Shiloh. 1 Kings 14: 1-18.

8. Give an account of the battle betweeen Jeroboam and Abijah. 2 Chron. 13.

9. How long did Jeroboam reign over Israel? 1 Kings 14: 20.

10. What do you know about Nadab's reign? 1 Kings 15: 25-28.

11. What do you know about Baasha and his reign? 1 Kings 15: 29-34; 2 Chron. 16: 1-6.

12. Give an account of the reign of Elah. 1 Kings 16: 8-10.

13. What do you know about Zimri and his reign? 1 Kings 16: 11-20.

14. How long was it after the death of Zimri before Omri became king? 1 Kings 16: 15-23.

15. What city did Omri build? 1 Kings 16: 24.

16. Where and how long did Omri reign? 1 Kings 16: 23, 24.

17. What further do you know about Omri? 1 Kings 16: 25-28.

18. What is said about Ahab's wickedness? 1 Kings 16: 29-33.

19. What wicked woman did he marry? 1 Kings 16: 31.

20. What great prophet appeared before Ahab, and what prophecy did he utter? 1 Kings 17: 1.

21. Give Elijah's experience at the brook Cherith. 1 Kings 17: 2-7.

22. Give an account of Elijah at Zarephath. 1 Kings 17: 8-24.

23. Give an account of the meeting and the conversation of Elijah and Obadiah. 1 Kings 18: 1-15.

24. Of what did Ahab accuse Elijah, and what was Elijah's answer? 1 Kings 18: 16-18.

25. Give an account of the contest at Mount Carmel. 1 Kings 18: 19-40.

26. Give an account of the rain that followed. 1 Kings 18: 41-46.

27. After this, why did Elijah flee? 1 Kings 19: 1-3.

28. Relate Elijah's experience under the juniper tree. 1 Kings 19: 4-8.

29. Give Elijah's experience at Mount Horeb. 1 Kings 19: 8-18.

30. Give an account of the meeting of Elijah and Elisha. 1 Kings 19: 19-21.

31. Give an account of the battle betweeen Ahab and Ben-hadad. 1 Kings 20: 1-21.

32. Tell about the next battle. 1 Kings 20: 22-30.

33. Why was Ahab rebuked by the prophet? 1 Kings 20: 35-43.

34. Give an account of Naboth and his vineyard. 1 Kings 21: 1-16.

35. Give an account of the meeting of Ahab and Elijah in Naboth's vineyard. 1 Kings 21: 17-26.

36. How was Ahab affected by Elijah's prophecy? 1 Kings 21: 27-29.

37. Give an account of Micaiah. 1 Kings 22: 1-28; 2 Chron. 18: 1-27.

38. Give an account of Ahab's death. 1 Kings 22: 29-40; 2 Chron. 18: 28-34.

39. What is said about Ahaziah? 1 Kings 22: 51-53.

40. Give an account of the sickness and death of Ahaziah. 2 Kings 1.

41. Give an account of Elijah's going into heaven. 2 Kings 2: 1-12.

42. On whom did Elijah's mantle fall? 2 Kings 2: 12-14.

43. Who searched for Elijah after his ascension? 2 Kings 2: 15-18.

(Lesson 21—Divided Kingdom—Continued)

1. What miracle did Elisha perform at Jericho? 2 Kings 2: 19-22.

2. Who called Elisha a "baldhead," and with what result? 2 Kings 2: 23-25.

3. What is said about Joram, or Jehoram? 2 Kings 3: 1-3.

4. Give an account of the miraculous appearance of water according to the word of Elisha. 2 Kings 3: 11-20.

5. How did Elisha bless the widow of one of the prophets? 2 Kings 4: 1-7.

6. Tell the story of the Shunammite woman. 2 Kings 4: 8-37.

7. Give an account of the poisonous pottage. 2 Kings 4: 38-41.

8. Give an account of the healing of Naaman, the leper. 2 Kings 5: 1-19.

9. Who was Gehazi, and what sin did he commit? 2 Kings 5: 20-27.

10. Give an account of the ax that was made to float. 2 Kings 6: 1-7.

11. Give an account of the Syrians being smitten blind. 2 Kings 6: 8-18.

12. How did Elisha treat these Syrians when he had led them to Samaria? 2 Kings 6: 20-23.

13. Tell about the great famine in Samaria. 2 Kings 6: 24-31.

14. How was the famine ended? 2 Kings 6: 32 to 7: 20.

15. After this, who was anointed to be king over Israel? 2 Kings 9: 1-10.

16. What two kings were killed in Naboth's vineyard? 2 Kings 9: 14-28.

17. Give an account of the death of Jezebel. 2 Kings 9: 29-37.

18. Tell of the further destruction of Ahab's family. 2 Kings 10: 1-17.

19. What did Jehu do to the worshipers of Baal? 2 Kings 10: 18-28.

20. What further do you know about Jehu? 2 Kings 10: 29-31.

5

21. What do you know about Jehoahaz and his reign? 2 Kings 13: 1-9.

22. Give an account of Jehoash and his reign. 2 Kings 13: 10-13.

23. Give an account of the death of Elisha. 2 Kings 13: 14-20.

24. Give an account of the battle between Jehoash and Amaziah. 2 Kings 14: 8-14.

25. What do you know about Jeroboam II. and his reign? 2 Kings 14: 23-29.

26. What do you know about Zechariah and his reign? 2 Kings 15: 8-12.

27. Tell what you know about Shallum and his reign. 2 Kings 15: 13-15.

28. Tell what you know about Menahem and his reign. 2 Kings 15: 17-22.

29. Give an account of Pekahiah and his reign. 2 Kings 15: 23-26.

30. Tell what you know about Pekah and his reign. 2 Kings 15: 27-31.

31. What do you know about Hoshea and his reign? 2 Kings 17: 1-6.

32. Why was Israel carried away into Assyrian captivity? 2 Kings 17: 7-23.

33. Who was sent to Samaria to repeople the cities? 2 Kings 17: 24, 25.

34. What do you know about these foreigners? 2 Kings 17: 27-41.

DRILL XII.—KINDOM OF JUDAH—Continued

From the Fall of Israel to the Fall of Judah

Scriptures covered, 2 Kings 21 to 25; 2 Chron. 33 to 36. From B.C. 722 to B.C. 587.   Time covered, 135 years.

THE KINGS OF JUDAH (CONTINUED)

14. MANASSEH.   2 Kings 12: 1-18.   (Idolatry is again introduced into Judah.)

15. AMON.   2 Kings 21: 19-26.   (Idolatry continues to flourish in Judah.)

16. JOSIAH.   2 Kings 22: 1 to 23: 30.   (Introduced many reforms; the last king to "walk in the ways of David.")

17. JEHOAHAZ.   2 Kings 23: 31-34.   (Dethroned by Pharaoh-necho of Egypt.)

18. JEHOIAKIM.   2 Kings 23: 36 to 24: 6.   (Tributary to Nebuchadnezzar; Daniel and his companions taken to Babylon.)   Dan. 1: 1-7.

19. JEHOIACHIN.   2 Kings 24: 8-17.   (Dethroned by Nebuchadnezzar; Ezekiel and ten thousand Jews are taken to Babylon.)   Ezek. 1: 1, 2.

20. ZEDEKIAH.   2 Kings 24: 18 to 25: 17.   (Dethroned by Nebuchadnezzar; Jerusalem and the temple are destroyed.)

PROPHETS

(a) Jeremiah.   (b) Ezekiel.   (c) Daniel.   (d) Obadiah. (Jeremiah, Ezekiel, and Zephaniah should be studied here.)

(Lesson 22—Kingdom of Judah—Continued)

1. Between what events is this period? See outline.
2. Between what dates is this period? See outline.
3. How long is this period? See outline.
4. What scriptures cover this period? See outline.
5. Who was Manasseh? 2 Kings 20: 21.
6. How old was he when he became king? 2 Kings 21: 1; 2 Chron. 33: 1.
7. How long did Manasseh reign? 2 Kings 21: 1; 2 Chron. 33: 1.
8. What do you know of Manasseh's wickedness? 2 Kings 21: 2-9; 2 Chron. 33: 2-9.
9. With what other sin is Manasseh charged? 2 Kings 21: 16; 24: 4.
10. On account of this wickedness what did Jehovah say he would do? 2 Kings 21: 10-15.
11. How did the Lord punish Manasseh? 2 Chron. 33: 10-13.
12. After this, what did Manasseh do? 2 Chron. 33: 14-17.
13. Who became king on the death of Manasseh? 2 Kings 21: 18.
14. How long did Amon reign? 2 Kings 21: 19; 2 Chron. 33: 21.
15. What do you know about Amon? 2 Kings 21: 21, 22.
16. In what respect did Amon differ from his father? 2 Chron. 33: 23.
17. How did Amon meet his death? 2 Kings 21: 23; 2 Chron. 33: 24.
18. How did the people avenge the death of Amon? 2 Kings 21: 24; 2 Chron. 33: 25.
19. Who reigned in Amon's stead? 2 Kings 21: 24; 2 Chron. 33: 25.
20. How old was Joash when he began to reign? 2 Kings 22: 1; 2 Chron. 34: 1.
21. How long did he reign? 2 Kings 22: 1; 2 Chron. 34: 1.
22. What kind of a king was Josiah? 2 Kings 22: 2; 23: 25; 2 Chron. 34: 2.

23. How old was Josiah when he began to seek Jehovah?
2 Chron. 34: 3.

24. How old was he when he began his reforms? 2 Chron.
34: 3.

25. Give an account of his purging Jerusalem and the land
of idolatry. 2 Chron. 34: 4-7.

26. After this, what great work did Josiah undertake? 2
Kings 22: 3-7; 2 Chron. 34: 8-13.

27. Who found the book of the law about this time? 2
Kings 22: 8-13; 2 Chron. 34: 14-21.

28. How was Josiah afflicted by the reading of the law? 2
Kings 22: 10-13; 2 Chron. 34: 19-21.

29. Of what prophetess did Josiah inquire? 2 Kings 22:
14; 2 Chron. 34: 22.

30. What message did Hulda send the king? 2 Kings
22: 15-20; 2 Chron. 34: 23-28.

31. What did Josiah do after this? 2 Kings 23: 1-14; 2
Chron. 34: 29-33.

32. After purging Jerusalem and Judea, what did Josiah
do? 2 Kings 23: 15, 16.

33. What prophet had told about this some three hundred
years before? 1 Kings 13: 1, 2.

34. What became of that prophet? 1 Kings 13: 3-32.

35. What do you know about the bones of this prophet?
2 Kings 23: 17, 18.

36. What did Josiah do in all the cities of Samaria? 2
Kings 23: 19, 20.

37. Give an account of the passover kept by Josiah. 2
Kings 23: 21-23; 2 Chron. 35: 1-19.

38. How did Josiah meet his death? 2 Kings 23: 29, 30;
2 Chron. 35: 20-24.

39. Who was the next king of Israel? 2 Kings 23: 30.

40. How long did Jehoahaz reign? 2 Kings 23: 31.

41. What kind of a king was he? 2 Kings 23: 32.

42. What king deposed Jehoahaz? 2 Kings 23: 33; 2
Chron. 36: 1-3.

43. Who was made king in his stead? 2 Kings 23: 34; 2
Chron. 36: 4.

44. Where did Jehoahaz die? 2 Kings 23: 34.

45. How long did Jehoiakim reign? 2 Kings 23: 36.

46. What do you know about him? 2 Kings 23: 37; 2 Chron. 36: 5.

47. What king did Jehoiakim serve for three years? 2 Kings 24: 1.

48. After this, what became of Jehoiakim, and why? 2 Kings 24: 1; 2 Chron. 36: 6, 7.

49. What do you know about his burial? Jer. 22: 18, 19; 36: 30.

50. What and who else were carried to Babylon at this time? 2 Chron. 36: 7; Dan. 1: 1-7.

51. Who was made king in Jehoiakim's stead? 2 Kings 24: 6.

52. How long did Jehoiakim reign? 2 Kings 24: 8.

53. What do you know about Jehoiachin and his reign? 2 Kings 24: 9-17.

54. Who and how many were carried into captivity at this time? 2 Kings 24: 14-16; Ezek. 1: 1, 2.

55. How did Jehoiachin fare in Babylon? 2 Kings 25: 27-30.

56. Who was the last king of Judah? 2 Kings 24: 17.

57. How long did Zedekiah reign? 2 Kings 24: 18.

58. What do you know about Zedekiah? 2 Kings 24: 19; 2 Chron. 36: 12, 13.

59. Describe the condition of Jerusalem at this time. 2 Chron. 36: 14-16.

60. Who besieged Jerusalem, and for how long? 2 Kings 25: 1-4.

61. How was Zedekiah punished? 2 Kings 25: 5-7.

62. Give an account of the destruction of Jerusalem. 2 Kings 25: 8-11; 2 Chron. 36: 17-21.

63. Who were left at Jerusalem, and for what purpose? 2 Kings 25: 12.

64. What became of the gold, silver, and the brass that belonged to the temple? 2 Kings 25 · 13-17.

65. After this, who was made ruler over Judah? 2 Kings 25: 22.

66. What became of Gedaliah? 2 Kings 25: 25.

67. After the death of Gedaliah. what did the people do, and why? 2 Kings 25: 26.

DRILL XIII.—BABYLONIAN CAPTIVITY
From Fall of Judah to Return to Jerusalem

Scriptures covered, 2 Kings 25: 8-21; Daniel 1-8.

From B.C. 587 to B.C. 537. Time covered, 50 years.

THE PARTIAL CAPTIVITIES

(a) The two and one-half tribes east of the Jordan. (b) The remainder of the "ten tribes." (c) Daniel and his companions. (d) Ezekiel and ten thousand Jews. (1 Chron. 5: 25, 26; 2 Kings 18: 9-12; Dan. 1: 1-7; 2 Kings 24: 10-17; Ezek. 1: 1; 2 Kings 17: 5, 6.)

THE GENERAL CAPTIVITY

(a) Jerusalem and the temple destroyed. (b) How long had the Jewish capital been at Jerusalem? (c) How old was the temple? (2 Kings 25.)

THE FOUR HEBREW CHILDREN

Give an account of Daniel, Shadrach, Meshach, and Abednego. (See Daniel, first chapter.)

NEBUCHADNEZZAR'S TWO DREAMS

(a) The great image and Daniel's interpretation. (b) The great tree and Daniel's interpretation. (See Daniel, chapters 2 and 4.)

NEBUCHADNEZZAR'S GOLDEN IMAGE

(a) Locate and describe the image. (b) Give an account of the dedication. (c) Shadrach, Meshach, and Abed-nego in the fiery furnace. (Dan. 3.)

THE FEAST OF BELSHAZZAR

(a) Give an account of the handwriting on the wall. (b) Give Daniel's interpretation. (Dan. 5.)

DANIEL IN THE LIONS' DEN

(a) Give the cause. (b) Give the result. (Dan. 6.) (Lamentations, and possibly Obadiah, should be read here.)

(Lesson 23—Babylonian Captivity)

1. Between what events is this period? See outline.
2. Between what dates is this period? See outline.
3. How long is this period? See outline.
4. What scriptures cover this period? See outline.
5. Give an account of the captivity of the two and one-half tribes east of the Jordan. 1 Chron. 5: 25, 26.
6. Give an account of the fall of Samaria. 2 Kings 17: 5, 6; 18: 9-11.
7. Why was Israel carried into captivity? 2 Kings 17: 7; 18: 12.
8. When were Daniel and his companions carried to Babylon? 2 Kings 24: 1-6; Dan. 1: 1-7.
9. How many Jews were carried away with Ezekiel? 2 Kings 24: 10-17; Ezek. 1: 1-3.
10. Give an account of the fall of Jerusalem. 2 Kings 24: 18 to 25: 17; 2 Chron. 36: 17-21.
11. Locate Babylon. It was situated on the Euphrates River, just north of the Persian Gulf.
12. Describe the city of Babylon. It was built on both sides of the Euphrates River, and was surrounded by a wall estimated to be more than three hundred feet high and some eighty-five feet thick. There were twenty-five large brass gates on each of the four sides of the wall. These opened into streets which cut the city into more than six hundred large blocks. (See Isa. 13: 19; also general history.)
13. What has become of this great Babylon? According to prophecy, it has been in ruins for many years.
14. Give the substance of Isaiah's prophecy. Isa. 13: 17-22.
15. Name the four "Hebrew children." Dan. 1: 6, 7.
16. How did Daniel display his courage at the first? Dan. 1: 5-8.
17. At the end of three years' preparation what is said about these boys? Dan. 1: 17-21.
18. Give an account of Nebuchadnezzar's decree to have all the wise men killed. Dan. 2: 1-13.
19. Why was this decree not carried out? Dan. 2: 14-24.
20. To whom did Daniel give the credit for the interpretation of this dream? Dan. 2: 25-30.

21. Relate Nebuchadnezzar's dream. Dan. 2: 31-35.
22. Give Daniel's interpretation of the dream. Dan. 2: 36-45.
23. What did the gold in the image represent? Nebuchadnezzar and the Babylonian kingdom.
24. What did the silver represent? The Persian kingdom.
25. What did the brass represent? The Grecian kingdom.
26. What did the iron represent? The Roman empire.
27. What did the stone "cut out without hands" represent? Dan. 2: 44, 45.
28. What reward did Daniel and his companions receive from Nebuchadnezzar? Dan. 2: 46-49.

(Lesson 24—Babylonian Captivity—Continued)

1. Give an account of the dedication of Nebuchadnezzar's golden image. Dan. 3: 1-7.
2. How did Shadrach, Meshach, and Abed-nego display their courage and loyalty to God at this dedication? Dan. 3: 8-18.
3. How did the king seek to punish them, and with what result? Dan. 3: 19-27.
4. After this, what did Nebuchadnezzar say and do? Dan. 3: 28-30.
5. Give an account of Nebuchadnezzar's dream found in Dan. 4: 4-18.
6. Give Daniel's interpretation of this dream. Dan. 4: 19-27.
7. How long was it until this was fulfilled? Dan. 4: 28-37.
8. Give an account of the "handwriting on the wall." Dan. 5: 1-9.
9. Who sought to comfort Belshazzar, and how? Dan. 5: 10-12.
10. Give the substance of Daniel's speech before Belshazzar. Dan. 5: 17-24.
11. What was the writing on the wall? Dan. 5: 25.
12. Give Daniel's interpretation. Dan. 5: 26-28.
13. How was Daniel rewarded for this? Dan. 5: 29.
14. What became of Belshazzar? Dan. 5: 30.
15. Who then received the kingdom? Dan. 5: 31. (It is

thought that Darius was only a temporary ruler until Cyrus could arrange to take the throne.)

16. How was Daniel promoted under Darius? Dan. 6: 1-3.

17. Why was Daniel cast into the lions' den? Dan. 6: 4-16.

18. How was Daniel protected from the lions? Dan. 6: 21, 22.

19. What became of the men who accused Daniel? Dan. 6: 24.

20. What decree did the king then make? Dan. 6: 25-27.

21. Relate Daniel's vision of the four beasts. Dan. 7: 1-8.

22. What did these four beasts represent? Dan. 7: 15-28.

23. Give Daniel's vision of the ram and the he-goat. Dan. 8: 1-14.

24. Give the interpretation of this vision. Dan. 8: 15-27.

DRILL XIV.—RESTORATION OF THE JEWS
From Return to Jerusalem to End of Old Testament History

Scriptures covered, Ezra, Nehemiah, Haggai, Zechariah, and Esther. (Dan. 9.)

From B.C. 537 to B.C. 445. Time covered, 92 years.

DANIEL'S PRAYER AND CONFESSION

(*a*) How did Daniel know it was time for the Jews to return? (*b*) Give the substance of Daniel's prayer. (*c*) Who answered this prayer? (See Dan. 9.)

THE DECREE OF CYRUS

(*a*) Who was Cyrus? (*b*) Why did he make this decree for the return of the Jews? (*c*) Who were required to assist the Jews, and how? (See Ez. 1.)

THE FIRST RETURN

UNDER ZERUBBABEL—50,000. (*a*) The temple rebuilt. (*b*) The Samaritans' proposition to assist rejected, and the result. (See Ez. 1 to 5.)

THE SECOND RETURN

UNDER EZRA—1,700. (*a*) Who was Ezra? (*b*) Of what sin did Ezra find the Jews guilty? (*c*) What reformation began at once? (See Ez. 7 to 10.)

THE THIRD RETURN

UNDER NEHEMIAH. (*a*) Who was Nehemiah? (*b*) Walls of Jerusalem rebuilt. (*c*) Give Nehemiah's experience with Sanballat. (*d*) Reformation continues. (See Neh. 1 to 13.)

THE STORY OF ESTHER

(*a*) Name the five principal characters in this story. (*b*) Give the story in brief. (Esth. 1 to 10.)

(Malachi should be studied here.)

(Lesson 25—Restoration of the Jews)

1. Define this period. It is the period during which the Jews returned from Babylon to Jerusalem.

2. Between what events is this period? See outline.

3. Between what dates is this period? See outline.

4. How long is this period? See outline.

5. How did Daniel know that it was time for the Jews to return? Dan. 9: 1, 2; Jer. 25: 11-14.

6. For what did Daniel pray? Dan. 9: 3-19.

7. Who answered Daniel's prayer? Dan. 9: 20-23.

8. Who made a decree allowing the Jews to return to Jerusalem? Ez. 1: 1-4.

9. What led Cyrus to make this decree? Ez. 1: 1.

10. How did Jehovah " stir up " the heart of Cyrus? Rollins says that Cyrus conversed freely with Daniel, and it is possible that Daniel showed him the prophecies where his name had been used in this connection more than one hundred years before, and in this way " stirred up " Cyrus' heart. Isa. 44: 28.

11. Who were required to assist the Jews in their return and in rebuilding the temple? Ez. 1: 3, 4, 6.

12. What did Cyrus furnish? Ez. 1: 7, 8.

13. How many of these vessels of gold and silver? Ez. 1: 11.

14. Who led the first company back to Jerusalem? Ez 2: 1, 2.

15. How many were in this company? Ez. 2: 3-65; Neh. 7: 66, 67.

16. How many beasts of burden had they? Ez. 2: 66, 67; Neh. 7: 68, 69.

17. About how long were these Jews en route from Babylon to Jerusalem? Ez. 7: 8, 9.

18. What was the first work after they reached Jerusalem? Ez. 3: 1-6.

19. When did they begin to rebuild the temple? Ez. 3: 8.

20. What did the people do when the foundation was laid? Ez. 3: 10, 11.

21. Why did the old men weep? Ez. 3: 12; Hag. 2: 3.

22. Who proposed to help rebuild the temple? Ez. 4: 1-10.

23. How was this proposition met? Ez. 4: 3.

24. How did these adversaries interfere with the work on the temple? Ez. 4: 4-24.

25. How long before they began the work again? Ez. 4: 24. [Twenty years (?).]

26. Through the influence of what two prophets was the work again taken up? Ez. 5: 1, 2; Hag. 1: 1, 2; Zech. 1: 1.

27. What effort was again made to interfere with the work? Ez. 5: 3-17.

28. What was the result of this effort? Ez. 6: 1-12.

29. When was this temple finally finished? Ez. 6: 15.

30. When the temple was finished, what did they do? Ez. 6: 16-18.

31. What feast was then observed? Ez. 6: 19-22.

32. Why did the Samaritans build them a temple, and where? They built a temple on Mount Gerizim, because they were not allowed to help the Jews rebuild the temple in Jerusalem.

33. Who led the second company back to Jerusalem? Ez. 7: 1-10.

34. How long was this after Zerubbabel's return? Ez. 1: 1; 7: 1-10. [Eighty years (?).]

35. How many were in Ezra's company? Ez. 8: 1-20.

36. Give the substance of the king's letter to the people. Ez. 7: 11-26.

37. What did this company do just before starting for Jerusalem? Ez. 8: 21-23.

38. What was done with the gold and silver, including vessels of gold and silver? Ez. 8: 24-30.

39. What was done with this gold and silver when they reached Jerusalem? Ez. 8: 31-34.

40. Of what sin did Ezra find the Jews guilty at Jerusalem? Ez. 9: 1-4.

41. Give the substance of Ezra's prayer. Ez. 9: 5-15.

42. How was the matter finally adjusted? Ez. 10: 1-14.

(Lesson 26—Restoration of the Jews—Continued)

1. How did Nehemiah learn of the condition of Jerusalem? Neh. 1: 1-3.

2. How long was this after Ezra went to Jerusalem? Ez 7: 7, 8; Neh. 2: 1. (Eleven years.)

3. How was Nehemiah affected when he heard that Jerusalem was still in ruins? Neh. 2: 1-3.

4. What request did he make of the king? Neh 2: 4-8.

5. What did Nehemiah do on arriving at Jerusalem? Neh. 2: 9-16.

6. What did he do next? Neh. 2: 17, 18.

7. What did Sanballat and Tobiah think of the effort to rebuild the walls of Jerusalem? Neh. 2: 19, 20; 4: 1-3.

8. What was the next effort of Sanballat and Tobiah? Neh. 4: 7, 8.

9. What did Nehemiah do then? Neh. 4: 9-14.

10. How did the Jews proceed with the work? Neh. 4: 15-23.

11. What trouble arose among the Jews at this time? Neh. 5: 1-5.

12. How was the matter finally adjusted? Neh. 5: 6-13.

13. How long was Nehemiah governor of Judea? Neh. 5: 14.

14. How did he treat these oppressed people? Neh. 5: 14-19.

15. When the walls were finished, what proposition did Sanballat, Tobiah, et al make to Nehemiah? Neh. 6: 1, 2.

16. What reply did Nehemiah make? Neh. 6: 3.

17. How often did they send to Nehemiah? Neh. 6: 4, 5.

18. Give the substance of Sanballat's letter to Nehemiah. Neh. 6: 5-7.

19. What answer did Nehemiah make? Neh. 6: 8.

20. Give Nehemiah's experience with Shemaiah. Neh. 6: 10-14.

21. How long did it take to repair the walls? Neh. 6: 15.

22. How can you account for the completion of the work in such a short time? Neh. 4: 6.

23. Give an account of Ezra's long sermon. Neh. 8: 1-12.

24. What did they find written in the law the next day? Neh. 8: 13-15.

25. How long did they continue to read and study the book of the law at this time? Neh. 8: 18.

26. What do you know about the public confession of their sins? Neh. 9: 4-37.

27. What covenant did Israel make at this time? **Neh. 9: 38 to 10: 39.**

28. What did they do with the mixed multitudes? **Neh. 13: 1-3.**

29. What do you know about Tobiah and the temple? **Neh. 13: 4-9.**

30. What else did Nehemiah find going wrong when he returned to Jerusalem? Neh. 13: 6, 10-31.

31. Tell how Esther became queen. Esth. 2: 1-18.

32. Tell how Mordecai saved the life of the king. Esth. 2: 19-23.

33. Give an account of the decree to have all the Jews killed. Esth. 3: 1-15.

34. How was this awful calamity averted? Esth. 4: 1 to 9: 19.

35. What institution was established to commemorate this great deliverance? Esth. 9: 20-32.

36. How was Mordecai promoted? Esth. 10.

DRILL XV.—BETWEEN THE TESTAMENTS
From Close of Old Testament to Opening of New Testament

Sources of information—Josephus, books of the Maccabees, general history.

Time covered, about 400 years. From B.C. 400 (?) to B.C. 4 (?).

THE PERSIAN RULE (SILVER EMPIRE)

(a) The first 137 years—before the close of the Old Testament. (b) The last 70 years—following the close of the Old Testament.

THE GRECIAN RULE (BRASS EMPIRE)

(a) The united kingdom, under Alexander the Great. (b) The divided kingdom (name and locate divisions). (c) The Holy Scriptures translated into Greek. (When? Where?)

THE JUDEAN INDEPENDENCE

(a) Antiochus Epiphanes introduces idolatry (40,000 Jews slaughtered). (b) The Maccabees. (1) Mattathias; (2) Judas, the hammer; (3) Eleazer, the beast sticker; (4) Jonathan, the cunning; (5) John, the holy; (6) Simon, the jewel; (7) John Hyrcanus.

THE ROMAN RULE (IRON EMPIRE)

(a) Pompey invades Judea. (b) Herod the Great made ruler over Judea. (c) The temple rebuilt at Jerusalem and at Samaria.

THE RISE OF THE SECTS

(a) Phariseees. (b) Sadducees. (c) Essenes. (d) Herodians. (e) Zealots.

(The Old Testament Apocrypha is thought to have been written during this period. It might be well to read it here.)

(Lesson 27—Between the Testaments)

1. Between what events is this period? See outline.
2. Between what dates is this period? See outline.
3. How many years does it cover? See outline.
4. To what people were the Jews tributary at the close of the Old Testament? The Persians.
5. How long had they been under the Persian rule? Since the days of Cyrus, about one hundred and thirty-seven years.
6. How much longer were they under the Persian rule? Until the time of Alexander the Great, about seventy years.
7. What is known of the Jews during these seventy years? The few facts that have come down to us indicate that the general trend of their course was downward.
8. To whom did the Jews next become tributary? The Greeks.
9. How long were they under the Grecian rule? Until the death of Alexander, about ten or twelve years.
10. How did the Jews fare under Alexander? He treated them kindly and respected their religion.
11. What city did Alexander build in Egypt? Alexandria.
12. With whom did he people this city? Greeks, Egyptians, and Jews.
13. What became of Alexander's kingdom at his death? It was divided among his four principal generals.
14. Name and locate these four kingdoms. The Western, or Macedonian; the Northern, or Armenian; the Eastern, or Syrian; the Southern, or Egyptian.
15. Under which of these were the Jews at the first? The Egyptian.
16. How long were the Jews under the Egyptian rule? About one hundred years.
17. How did they fare during this time? Fairly well, it is thought. Their history during these one hundred years is dull.
18. Which of the kingdoms next exercised authority over the Jews? The Syrian.
19. How did they fare under the Syrian rule? Very badly indeed.
20. Who was Antiochus Epiphanes? One of the Syrian kings.

21. What do you know about him?   The historian says:
"Into the eleven years of his reign (175-164 B.C.) were
crowded such horrors as have seldom disgraced a sovereign or
maddened a people."

22. How did he offend the Jews?   He made a decree for-
bidding them to worship Jehovah.

23. How else did he offend them?   He introduced idolatry
into Jerusalem, sacrificed a sow on the altar, and even made
a broth of some of the meat and besmeared the temple with it.

24. How many Jews were slaughtered in an attempt to
force them into idolatry?   Forty thousand.

25. What aged priest began the war for independence?
Mattathias.

26. Give the names of his five sons.   Judas, the hammer
(called "Judas Maccabeus"); Jonathan, the cunning; John,
the holy; Eleazer, the beast sticker; and Simon, the jewel.

27. How many Jews perished rather than resist on the
Sabbath day?   One thousand.

28. On the death of Mattathias, who became the leader?
Judas, the third son.

29. Give an account of the career of Judas Maccabeus.
With a small army he soon rescued Jerusalem from the Syrians.   He cleansed the temple and reëstablished the divine
worship.   He had five splendid victories in rapid succession.

30. How did Judas die?   He finally fell on the battle-
field, with his back to the ground and his face to the enemy.

31. Why was Eleazer called the "beast sticker?"   When
the Syrians entered Palestine with twenty large elephants,
Eleazer discovered one that was larger and more gorgeously
decorated than the rest.   He supposed that the king was rid-
ing on this beast, and broke through the line of guards, ran
under the beast, and thrust his sword into his body, killing
the beast, himself, and many others.

32. On the death of Judas, who became the leader?   Jonathan.

33. How did John meet his death?   Jonathan sent John,
with the women and children, beyond the Jordan, while he
pushed the war for independence.   The Arabs treacherously
slew John, thus violating their first law—to "show kindness
to strangers."

34. What important change occurred in the time of Jonathan? The office of the high priest was transferred from the family of Aaron to the Maccabean family, Jonathan becoming high priest.

35. How did the independence cause prosper under Jonathan? Splendidly.

36. How did Jonathan finally meet his death? He was led into a trap by Tryphon, the great "king maker," and thus became a prisoner. Tryphon promised to release him on the receipt of a large sum of money. Simon, his brother, sent the ransom money. Tryphon kept the money and slew his prisoner.

37. After the death of Jonathan, who became the leader? Simon, the eldest son of Mattathias.

38. Was Simon also proclaimed high priest? He was.

39. When did· the Jews gain their independence? Under Simon, in the year 142 B.C., by a treaty of peace.

(Lesson 28—Between the Testaments—Continued)

1. How long had they been in subjection to other nations? Since they were carried away to Babylon, three hundred and sixty-five years.

2. How long did this independence last? Less than one hundred years.

3. Give an account of the happy state during Simon's reign. The historian says: "Every man tilled his land with peace; and the land yielded her increase, and the trees of the field their fruit. Every man sat under his vine and under his fig tree, and there was none to make them afraid. The land had rest and the people had plenty."

4. How did Simon seek the favor of Rome? He sent an embassy to cultivate Rome's friendship, and also sent as a present a shield of gold weighing more than one thousand pounds.

5. In his old age how did Simon meet his death? His son-in-law, Ptolemy, conceived the idea of making himself ruler by exterminating the Maccabean family. He murdered Simon and his oldest son, Judas, and held Simon's wife and the two younger sons as prisoners. (John, another son, escaped.)

6. Who took the lead after Simon's death? John Hyrcanus, the son of Simon, who escaped death at the hands of his
brother-in-law, Ptolemy.

7. What became of Simon's wife and the two sons? John
raised an army and besieged the stronghold where Ptolemy
held them as prisoners. Ptolemy exposed them on the wall,
threatening to kill them if John did not raise the siege; and
although his mother pleaded with him to avenge the death of
her husband and his father, the sight of his mother and two
brothers moved John to withdraw his army. Then Ptolemy
slew his prisoners and fled beyond the Jordan.

8. What do you know of the reign of John Hyrcanus? He
reigned prosperously for twenty-nine years, and his kingdom
increased until it approached the glory and extent of Solomon's kingdom.

9. What two enemies did John subdue? The Samaritans
and the Edomites.

10. What do you know about John and the temple on
Mount Gerizim? John destroyed this temple after it had
stood about two hundred years. It was never rebuilt.

11. Relate the conversation between Jesus and the Samari-
tan woman. John 4: 1-26.

12. On the death of John Hyrcanus, who became leader?
His son, Aristobulus.

13. What is said about Aristobulus and his reign? "He
reigned only one year, but into this one year he crowded
enough crime to make himself unique in infamy."

14. Who next became the leader? Jonathan, a brother of
Aristobulus.

15. What do you know of his reign? The historian says:
"His reign of twenty-seven years is one long story of border
and civil war, of alternate success and defeat, of daring ad-
venture and ruthless slaughter."

16. Who came to the throne on the death of Jonathan?
His wife, Alexandria.

17. What is said of her reign? She is said to have held the
reins of the government wisely and firmly.

18. On the death of Alexandria, what happened? The
Jews at this time had become divided into the two great religious sects, Pharisees and Sadducees. The two sons of Alex-

andria, Aristobulus and Hyrcanus, each aspired to the throne. One was a Pharisee and the other a Sadducee; and, as a result, civil war broke out.

19. What finally became of this civil strife? Both the sons appealed to Rome for help; and, in response, Rome sent an army under Pompey to invade Judea. The strife continued a number of years, and finally ended by the Jews becoming tributary to Rome. Thus ended their brief independence.

20. When did Herod become governor of Judea? In B.C. 40.

21. Who was Herod? He was a descendant of the Edomites.

22. What do you know about the character of Herod? He was wicked, envious, jealous, and cruel.

23. What do you know of his wife, Mariamne? She was a descendant of the Maccabean family, and was said to be the most beautiful woman of the age.

24. What became of Mariamne? Jealous of her lest she should seek to turn the kingdom over to the Maccabean family, Herod ordered her killed.

25. What other crimes did he commit against the Maccabean family? He killed Mariamne's father, grandfather, and uncle; and, fearing that her two sons (his own sons as well) would seek the throne, he ordered a mock trial for them and had them condemned and killed.

26. Who was partly responsible for these awful crimes? Herod's sister, Salome, who is said to have aroused and kept alive his jealousy.

27. What awful crime is recorded against him in the Bible? Matt. 2: 16.

28. Do you know anything more of Herod's wickedness? In order that there might be general mourning when he died, he ordered the chief men of the Jews to be imprisoned, and gave order to Salome and her husband to have the soldiers kill them as soon as the breath left his body. This scheme was devised while he was on his deathbed.

29. How did the Jews feel toward Herod? They hated him heartily, of course.

30. How did he attempt to regain their friendship in his old days? By tearing down the temple that Zerubbabel built

(which had never been satisfactory to the Jews) and building
it on a more magnificent scale.

31. How did Heroed die? He died of a loathsome dis-
ease, with " not one soul in all the earth to love him or to
weep for him."

32. Name the Jewish sects. Pharisees, Sadducees, Essenes,
Herodians, and Zealots.

33. When did these sects arise? During the period between the Testaments.

34. What did the Pharisees believe? They believed in angels and spirits and in the resurrection. They also accepted
tradition, or " the unwritten law," as authority in religious
matters.

35. What did the Sadducees believe? They did not believe
in angels, spirits, or the resurrection; and they did not ac-
cept tradition, or " the unwritten law." (See Acts 23: 8.)

36. Who were the Essenes? They were a class of Jews
that made purity of life their one great object. They also
believed in holding " all things in common."

37. Who were the Herodians? A sect among the Jews
who supported the Herodian family in the hope of maintain-
ing their independence.

38. Who were the Zealots? A sect of the Jews who took
into their own hands, without due process of law, the punish-
ment of flagrant offenses.

39. Name the Apocryphal books of the Old Testament.
I Esdras, II Esdras, Tobit, Judith, Additions to the Book of
Esther, the Wisdom of Solomon, the Wisdom of Jesus (or
Ecclesiasticus), Baruch, the Song of the Three Holy Children,
the History of Susanna, Bel and the Dragon, the Prayer of
Manasses (king of Judah), I Maccabees, II Maccabees.

40. What does the word "Apocrypha" mean? It literally means " hidden."

41. Why are these books not a part of our Bible? No
one knows when nor by whom they were written.

42. When are they supposed to have been written? Some
time during the period between the Testaments.

43. Name the books of the New Testament Apocrypha.
Mary, Protevangelion, I Infancy, II Infancy, Christ and
Angarus, the Apostles' Creed, Laodiceans, Paul and Seneca,

Paul and Theola, I Corinthians, II Corinthians, Barnabas, Ephesians, Magnesians, Trallians, Romans, Philadelphians, Smyrnaseans, Polycarp, Philippians, I Hermas, II Hermas, III Hermas.

44. When are these supposed to have been written? During the first four centuries after Christ.

45. How should these Apocryphal books of the Old and the New Testaments be received? As the writings of uninspired men, as secular history.

DRILL XVI.—THE LIFE OF CHRIST
From the Birth of Christ to the Ascension
Scriptures covered, Matt. 1 to John 21.

From B.C. 4 to A.D. 30. Time covered, 34 years.

JOHN THE BAPTIST

(a) Prophecy relating to John. (b) His mission. (c) His message. (d) Was John the Baptist Elijah? (See Matt. 17: 1-13.) (Isa. 40: 3-5; Matt. 3: 1-17; Luke 3: 1-20; Matt. 14: 1-12.)

JESUS, FROM HIS BIRTH TO HIS BAPTISM

(a) "The song of the angels." (b) The visit of the wise men. (c) Herod's wicked edict. (d) Flight and return; his home at Nazareth. (e) The visit to Jerusalem. (f) His occupation. (g) His baptism: Where? How? Why? (Matt. 1 to 3; Mark 1: 1-11; Luke 2: 1 to 3: 22.)

FROM HIS BAPTISM TO THE TRANSFIGURATION

(a) His temptation. (b) The Sermon on the Mount. (c) The twelve and seventy sent out. (d) The transfiguration: Where? What? (Matt. 4 to 17; Mark 1: 12 to 9: 13; Luke 4: 1 to 9: 36.)

FROM THE TRANSFIGURATION TO THE CRUCIFIXION

(a) The last passover. (b) The Supper is instituted. (c) The Lord's Prayer. (d) In the garden. (e) His trials. (f) The crucifixion. (Matt. 26: 17 to 27: 44; Mark 14: 12 to 15: 32.)

FROM THE CRUCIFIXION TO THE ASCENSION

(a) His burial. (b) His resurrection. (c) Appearances after his resurrection. (d) The great commission. (e) The ascension. (Matt. 27: 57 to 28: 20; Mark 15: 42 to 16: 20; 1 Cor. 15: 1-8.)

(Lesson 29—John the Baptist)

1. Who was John the Baptist? Luke 1: 13; John 1: 6.
2. Was John a prophet? Matt. 11: 9.
3. Was John a Christian? Matt. 3: 3.
4. Was John a member of the church? Matt. 11: 11.
5. Describe John's raiment. Matt. 3: 4.
6. What kind of food did John eat? Matt. 3: 4.
7. What was John's mission in the world? John 1: 1-7.
8. What did John teach respecting the kingdom? Matt. 3: 2.
9. What does the expression "at hand" mean? 2 Tim. 4: 6.
10. What was the personal name of the Baptist? John 1: 6.
11. Why, then, was he called "the Baptist?" Because he baptized.
12. Is any one else ever called "Baptist" in the Bible? No.
13. Where did John baptize? Matt. 3: 5, 6.
14. Why was John baptizing in Ænon? John 3: 23.
15. For what did John baptize? Luke 3: 3.
16. What great character did John baptize? Matt. 3: 13-16.
17. Why was Jesus baptized? Matt. 3: 15.
18. Did John feel worthy to baptize Jesus? Matt. 3: 14-16.
19. What comparison did he make between Jesus and himself? John 3: 27-31.
20. Was John's baptism to continue? Acts 10: 36, 37; 18: 24-26; 19: 1-6.
21. Did John perform any miracles? John 10: 41.
22. Who imprisoned John, and why? Matt. 14: 3, 4.
23. Who beheaded John, and why? Matt. 14: 6-11.
24. Who buried John? Matt. 14: 12.
25. Was John with Jesus on the mount of transfiguration? Matt. 17: 9-13; Mal. 4: 5, 6; Luke 1: 13-17; Matt. 11: 14; John 1: 19-21.

(Lésson 30—From Birth to Baptism)

1. How long had Jesus existed before he was born into the world? John 1: 1-4; 8: 58; 17: 5.

2. Where was Jesus born? Matt. 2: 1-6.

3. What king had been born there about one thousand years before? 1 Sam. 17: 12.

4. Locate Bethlehem. See the map.

5. Why did Joseph and Mary go to Bethlehem? Luke 2: 1-4.

6. To whom did the angels sing when Jesus was born? Luke 2: 8-14.

7. What were these shepherds doing at the time? Luke 2: 8.

8. Do shepherds watch their flocks at night there on December 25? Improbable.

9: Then is it probable that Jesus was born on December 25? It is not.

10. By whose authority is December 25 celebrated as the birthday of Jesus? By the authority of the Roman Catholic Church.

11. What other day is observed by the same authority? Easter Sunday.

12. Do you think God intended for us to observe these days; and if not, why not? The Bible is silent on the subject.

13. Who came from the East to worship the young child? Matt. 2: 1.

14. How did they know the child had been born? Matt. 2: 2.

15. Who instructed the "wise men" to bring him word where the child was? Matt. 2: 7, 8.

16. Why did Herod wish to know where the child was? Matt. 2: 13.

17. What did the "wise men" do about it, and why? Matt. 2: 12.

18. What did Herod then seek to do? Matt. 2: 16.

19. What do you know about the character of Herod? See Questions 60 to 65 in "Between the Testaments."

20. How long had Herod been governor of Judea? See Question 59, "Between the Testaments."

21. By whose authority did he hold this office? The Roman Government.

22. How was the child Jesus saved out of Herod's hand? Matt. 2: 13-15.

23. How long did Joseph and Mary and Jesus remain in Egypt? Matt. 2: 15.

24. What direction is Egypt from Bethlehem? See the map.

25. Where was Joseph and Mary's home after they returned from Egypt? Matt. 2: 19-23.

26. Why did they not return to Judea from Egypt? Matt. 2: 22.

27. Locate Nazareth. See the map.

28. How long did Jesus make Nazareth his home? Matt. 13: 54-58 (Matt. 4: 12, 13).

29. Are there any prophecies relating to his dwelling at Nazareth? Matt. 2: 23 (see also John 1: 46).

30. Where did Jesus make his home after he was rejected at Nazareth? Matt. 4: 12, 13.

31. Locate Capernaum. See the map.

32. How old was Jesus the first time he was in Jerusalem? Luke 2: 21-28 (Lev. 12: 1-5).

33. How old was he the next time we hear of him at Jerusalem? Luke 2: 42.

34. Why did he go up to Jerusalem at this time? Luke 2: 41, 42.

35. How often did Joseph and Mary go up to Jerusalem? Luke 2: 41.

36. What was Jesus' occupation before he began preaching? Matt. 13: 55; Mark 6: 3.

37. Where and by whom was Jesus baptized? Matt. 3: 13-15.

38. Were Jesus and John related; and if so, how? Luke 1: 36.

39. Which was the older, Jesus or John, and how much? Luke 1: 36.

40. What did John say about baptizing Jesus? Matt. 3: 13, 14.

41. For what was Jesus baptized? Matt. 3: 15.

42. How did God publicly acknowledge Jesus after his baptism? Matt. 3: 16, 17.

43. How old was Jesus when he was baptized? Luke 3: 21-23.

44. How far did Jesus probably walk to be baptized? Matt. 3: 13.

45. What does the name "Immanuel" mean? Matt. 1: 23.

(Lesson 31—From Baptism to Transfiguration)

1. How long did Jesus fast in the wilderness? Matt. 4: 1, 2.

2. How then was he tempted? Matt. 4: 2, 3.

3. How did Jesus answer the devil? Matt. 4: 4.

4. In what way was he next tempted? Matt. 4: 5, 6.

5. What answer did Jesus make this time? Matt. 4: 7.

6. Where and how was he next tempted? Matt. 4: 8, 9.

7. What did Jesus answer this time? Matt. 4: 10.

8. How was Jesus comforted after his temptation? Matt. 4: 11.

9. What message did Jesus preach? Matt. 4: 17.

10. Had this ever been preached before? Matt. 3: 1, 2.

11. What three chapters in Matthew record the Sermon on the Mount? Matt. 5 to 7.

12. On what mountain was this sermon preached? Supposed to be the "Horns of Hattin," a mountain seven miles south of Capernaum.

13. Name the "Beatitudes." Matt. 5: 3-12.

14. Mention five other things taught in the Sermon on the Mount. Matt. 5 to 7.

15. What lesson did Jesus teach by referring to the lilies? Matt. 6: 28-30.

16. What did Jesus say about judging others? Matt. 7: 1-5.

17. What did he teach about entering the kingdom? Matt. 7: 21.

18. What lesson did Jesus teach about building on the rock and on the sand? Matt. 7: 24-27.

19. How many disciples did Jesus send out the first time? Matt. 10: 1-6.

20. Are these the same twelve that were later sent into all the world? Acts 1: 15-26.

21. What were these twelve told to preach? Matt. 10: 7.

22. To whom were they told to preach? Matt. 10: 5, 6.

(Lesson 32—From Baptism to Transfiguration— Continued)

1. How many disciples did Jesus afterwards send out? Luke 10: 1.

2. What were they told to preach? Luke 10: 9.

3. To whom were they told to preach? Luke 10: 1.

4. Who first preached "the kingdom is at hand?" Matt. 3: 1, 2.

5. What had Daniel said about the kingdom? Dan. 2: 44.

6. Was the kingdom here when Jesus taught his disciples to pray? Matt. 6: 9, 10.

7. Was the kingdom here while Jesus was on the cross? Luke 23: 42.

8. Was the kingdom here when Jesus died? Luke 23: 50, 51.

9. Was the kingdom here when Jesus ascended? Acts 1: 6.

10. Did Jesus ever sit on David's literal throne on earth? Of course not.

11. Who was the last king to sit on David's throne? See "Kingdom of Judah—Continued."

12. When was Jesus crowned king? Acts 2: 22-36.

13. Give Matthew's description of the transfiguration. Matt. 17: 1-8.

14. Give Mark's account of it. Mark 9: 2-8.

15. Give Luke's statement of the transfiguration. Luke 9: 28-36.

16. Who went up on the mountain with Jesus? Matt. 17: 1.

17. What did Peter say when he saw Jesus transfigured and Moses and Elijah with him? Matt. 17: 4.

18. How long had Moses been dead? About fifteen hundred years.

19. How did Peter know this was Moses? Matt. 17: 3; Mark 9: 4; Luke 9: 30.

20. Who was this Elijah? Matt. 17: 9-13; Mal. 4: 5, 6; Luke 1: 13-17; Matt. 11: 11-14 (?).

21. What did the voice out of heaven say to Peter? Matt. 17: 5.

22. What was the object of the transfiguration? Matt. 17: 5; Luke 9: 33-35.

23. On what mountain was Jesus transfigured? Mount Hermon (?).

(Lesson 33—From Transfiguration to Crucifixion)

1. Where did Jesus eat the last passover with his disciples? Luke 22: 7-12.

2. Name the three annual feasts of the Jews. Passover, Pentecost, and tabernacles.

3. Where did the passover originate, and why called a "passover?" In Egypt. Because the death angel passed over the houses where the Israelites were.

4. On what day of the month did they observe the passover? Josh. 5: 10.

5. By what other name is the feast of passover called? Luke 22: 1.

6. Who did Jesus send to make ready the passover? Mark 14: 12, 13; Luke 22: 7, 8.

7. Who ate the passover with Jesus? Matt. 26: 20; Mark 14: 17.

8. After the passover, what institution was established? Matt. 26: 26-29.

9. Did all the disciples eat the Lord's Supper? Matt. 26: 26-29; Mark 14: 17-25; Luke 22: 14-23 [John 13: 21-30 (?)].

10. After the Supper, what discourse did Jesus deliver? John 14, 15, 16.

11. After this, what prayer did Jesus pray? John 17.

12. After the discourse and the prayer, where did they go? John 18: 1.

13. Where was the garden of Gethsemane? John 18: 1.

14. Did Jesus often visit this garden? John 18: 2.

15. Did all the disciples go into the garden? Matt. 26: 36, 37; Mark 14: 32, 33.

16. What three disciples went into the midst of the garden with him? Matt. 26: 36, 37.

17. Give the substance of Jesus' prayer in the garden. Matt. 26: 39-44.

18. Describe his agony in the garden. Luke 22: 44.

19. What were the disciples doing while Jesus was praying? Luke 22: 45.

20. Who led the mob into the garden to seek Jesus? Matt. 26: 47; John 18: 3.

21. How did Judas make Jesus known to the mob? Matt. 26: 48, 49; Mark 14: 44, 45.

22. How did Peter attempt to defend Jesus? John 18: 10.

23. What did Jesus say and do? Matt. 26: 52; Luke 22: 50, 51.

24. Before whom did the mob take Jesus? John 18: 12, 13.

25. Who was Annas? John 18: 13.

26. To whom did Annas send Jesus? John 18: 24.

(Lesson 34—From Transfiguration to Crucifixion—Continued)

1. How did Peter follow Jesus at this time? Matt. 26: 58; Mark 14: 54.

2. Relate the circumstances of Peter's denial. Mark 14: 66-72.

3. To whom did Caiaphas send Jesus? John 18: 28, 29.

4. What kind of trial had he undergone up to this time? Ecclesiastical.

5. Why was Jesus carried before Pilate? John 18: 31.

6. What accusations did they bring against Jesus? Luke 23: 1-5.

7. To whom did Pilate send Jesus? Luke 23: 6, 7.

8. Who was this Herod? Matt. 14: 1; Luke 3: 1.

9. How did Herod treat Jesus? Luke 23: 8-11.

10. What did Herod then do with Jesus? Luke 23: 11.

11. What was Pilate's conclusion after hearing all the accusations? Matt. 27: 11-25; Mark 15: 1-15; John 18: 29-40.

12. Why, then, did Pilate deliver him up to be crucified? Mark 15: 15.

13. What word did Pilate's wife send him? Matt. 27: 19.

7

14. Who was compelled to carry his cross?   Mark 15: 21;
Luke 23: 26.

15. Where was Jesus crucified?   Mark 15: 22.

16. Who was crucified with Jesus?   Luke 23: 32.

17. Mention Jesus' sayings on the cross.   Matt. 27: 46;
Mark 15: 34; Luke 23: 34-43; John 19: 25-30.

18. On what day of the week was Jesus crucified?   Matt.
27: 62-66; John 18: 28.

19. Who buried Jesus?   John 19: 38-40.

20. Where was Jesus buried?   Matt. 27: 59, 60; John 19:
41, 42.

21. What precaution did the priests and Pharisees take to
prevent the disciples from stealing the body?   Matt. 27:
62-66.

22. What sentence was written over Jesus' head?   Matt.
27: 37.

23. What became of Judas?   Matt. 27: 3-10; Acts 1: 18

24. Was Judas a devil from the beginning?   John 13: 2,
27; 6: 64.

(Lesson 35—From Crucifixion to Ascension)

1. Was the resurrection of Jesus a matter of prophecy?
Ps. 16: 10; Acts 2: 25-31.

2. Had Jesus told the disciples of the resurrection?   Matt.
16: 21.

3. Did the disciples believe Jesus would rise from the
dead?   John 20: 9.

4. On what day did Jesus rise?   Mark 16: 9.

5. What time of the day was it?   Mark 16: 9.

6. What difficulty were the women discussing as they
neared the tomb?   Mark 16: 3.

7. Who had rolled the stone away?   Matt. 28: 2.

8. Who was this angel?   Mark 16: 5.

9. What do Luke and John say about it?   Luke 24: 4;
John 20: 12.

10. What does the word "angel" mean?   It comes from
the Greek word "angelos," and signifies "messenger."

11. Can you give another instance where men are called
"angels?"   Gen. 18 and 19.

12. To whom did Jesus first appear after his resurrection? Mark 16: 9.

13. Give the different times and places where he appeared to his disciples after his resurrection. Matt. 28; Mark 16; Luke 24; John 20, 21; 1 Cor. 15: 1-8.

14. Who was the last person to see Jesus? 1 Cor. 15: 8.

15. What did the chief priests and elders do when they heard of the resurrection of Jesus? Matt. 28: 11-15.

16. Did the Jews generally believe the disciples' report or the false report of the soldiers? Matt. 28: 15.

17. Did the disciples themselves believe when they first heard of the resurrection? Mark 16: 12-14.

18. What became of Jesus' spirit while the body was in the tomb? Acts 2: 25-31.

19. What does the Greek word "Hades" mean? "The unseen world."

20. What Hebrew word in the Old Testament means the same thing? Ps. 16: 10 ("Sheol").

21. Did the same body that was buried come out of the tomb? Luke 24: 39, 40.

22. Where had Jesus told his disciples that he would meet them after his resurrection? Matt. 26: 31, 32.

23. What information did the angels at the tomb give the women? Matt. 28: 7.

24. What did the disciples do? Matt. 28: 16.

25. Locate Galilee. John 4: 1, 2. (See map.)

(Lesson 36—From Crucifixion to Ascension— Continued)

1. At what place in Galilee did Jesus meet them? Matt. 28: 16.

2. Repeat the "great commission" as given by Matthew. Matt. 28: 18-20.

3. Repeat the commission as given by Mark. Mark 16: 15, 16.

4. Repeat the commission as given by Luke. Luke 24: 46, 47.

5. What does John say about the commission? John 20: 21-23.

6. Why is this called the "great commission?" See above.

7. What part of this commission binds the church? Mark 16: 15; Matt. 28: 18-20.

8. What part binds the sinner? Mark 16: 16.

9. What is the Lord's part? Mark 16: 16.

10. After giving the apostles the commission, where did he tell them to "tarry?" Luke 24: 49.

11. Why were they to wait at Jerusalem? Luke 24: 48-53.

12. Are there any prophecies relating to Jerusalem and the word of the Lord? Isa. 2: 1, 2; Mic. 4: 1-3.

13. When did these apostles receive the Holy Spirit? Acts 2: 1-4.

14. Is there any prophecy relating to the outpouring of the Holy Spirit? Joel 2: 28-30.

15. What is the meaning of "all flesh?" Gal. 2: 16; Luke 2: 30-32; 3: 6.

16. When did the Gentiles receive the baptism of the Holy Spirit? Acts 10: 36-44.

17. What "signs" did Jesus say would follow them that believe? Mark 16: 17, 18.

18. Give some instances where the "signs" did follow. Acts 2: 4; 3: 1-10; 5: 12-16; 8: 6; 10: 44-46; 19: 1-6; 28: 1-6.

19. What was the purpose of these "signs?" Mark 16: 20; Heb. 2: 4; John 3: 1-3.

20. What has become of these "signs," or "spiritual gifts?" 1 Cor. 12 to 14.

21. Had Jesus told the disciples of his ascension? John 14: 1-3.

22. From what place did Jesus ascend? Acts 1: 12.

23. Where did the disciples go after the ascension? Acts 1: 12.

24. How long was it between the crucifixion and the ascension? Acts 1: 1-3.

DRILL XVII.—CHURCH OF GOD
From the Ascension to the Death of Paul
Scriptures covered, Acts to Revelation.
From A.D. 30 to A.D. 100.   Time covered, 70 years.

THE CHURCH DEFINED

(a) The family of God.   (b) The spiritual body of Christ.
(c) The called out.   (1 Tim. 3: 15; Eph. 1: 22, 23.)

THE MOTHER CHURCH AT JERUSALEM

(a) The disciples at Jerusalem.   (b) The day of Pentecost.   (c) Baptism of the Holy Spirit.   (d) Peter's sermon.
(e) The results.   (f) The first persecution.   (g) The second persecution.   (h) The first Christian martyr.   (Acts 1
to 7.)

CHURCH EXTENDED BY SCATTERED DISCIPLES

(a) In Phenicia.   (b) In Cyprus.   (c) In Antioch.
Acts 8: 1, 2; 11: 19.

CHURCH EXTENDED BY PHILIP

(a) In Samaria.   (b) To the eunuch.   (c) In Cesarea.
(Acts 8: 5-40; 21: 7-10.)

CHURCH EXTENDED BY PETER

(a) The visions of Cornelius and Peter.   (b) Peter's sermon.   (c) The result.   (d) The baptism of the Holy Spirit
—its design?   (Acts 10 and 11.)

CHURCH EXTENDED BY PAUL

(a) His conversion.   (b) Visits Jerusalem.   (c) Goes to
Antioch.   (d) First missionary journey.   (e) The second
journey.   (f) The third journey.   (g) Apprehended at Jerusalem.   (h) His experience at Cesarea.   (i) His voyage
to Rome.

(Lesson 37—Definition and Mother Church)

1. Where did the apostles go after the ascension of Jesus?
Acts 1: 12.
2. Why did they go to Jerusalem?   Luke 24: 49.
3. What had Jesus promised to send them?   Acts 1: 4, 5.
4. Where did they wait in Jerusalem?   Luke 24: 53.
5. How many days did they wait there?   Acts 1: 1-5.
6. What business did they transact during these days?
Acts 1: 16-26.
7. When did they receive the baptism of the Holy Spirit?
Acts 2: 1-4.
8. Who had foretold the outpouring of the Holy Spirit?
Joel 2: 28.
9. Describe this baptism of the Holy Spirit.   Acts 2: 1-4.
10. Who received this baptism of the Holy Spirit?   Acts
1: 26; 2: 1-4.
11. What other case of the Holy-Spirit baptism is recorded?
Acts 10: 44.
12. How did others receive the Spirit in those days?   Acts
8: 14-17; 19: 1-6.
13. Could just any preacher impart the Spirit?   Acts 8:
14-17; 19: 1-6.
14. Could any one except an apostle impart the Spirit?
Acts 9: 17.
15. How do people receive the Spirit now?   Eph. 5: 18,
19; Col. 3: 16.
16. What does the word "church" mean?   It comes from
the Greek word "ekklesia," and means a called-out company.
17. What does Paul tell us the church is?   Eph. 1: 22, 23;
Col. 1: 18, 24.
18. How many bodies are there?   Rom. 12: 4, 5; 1 Cor.
12: 12-20; Eph. 4: 4.

(Lesson 38—Definition and Mother Church—
Continued)

1. In 1 Tim. 3: 14, 15, what does Paul say the church is?
2. Then how many families, or houses, has God?   One,
of course.

3. Must one be a child of God to be saved?   Rom. **8:** 17, 18.

4. Can one be a child of God and not be in his family, or house?   No.

5. Then can one be saved without being a member of the church?   (John 3: 3-5.)

6. What scriptural names are applied to the church?   Rom. 16: 16; 1 Cor. 1: 1, 2.

7. Give the substance of Peter's sermon on Pentecost. Acts 2: 14-36.

8. Why did Peter not preach "the kingdom is at hand?" Col. 1: 13.

9. Should we now pray for the kingdom to come?   Matt. 6: 10.

10. What effect did Peter's sermon have on the people? Acts 2: 37.

11. What question did they ask?   Acts 2: 37.

12. Give Peter's answer to this question.   Acts 2: 38.

13. What is meant by "the gift of the Holy Spirit?" Acts 2: 38.

14. To whom is the promise (of salvation) made?   Acts 2: 39 (Tit. 2: 11).

15. How many disciples were added that day?   Acts 2: 41.

16. How many believers were there soon after this?   Acts 4: 4.

(Lesson 39—Definition and Mother Church— Continued)

1. What noted miracle did Peter perform about this time? Acts 3: 1-10.

2. How were Peter and John treated at this time?   Acts 4: 1-3.

3. Give an account of their trial the next day.   Acts 4: 5-22.

4. When they were liberated, what did they do?   Acts 4: 23-31.

5. What great sin did Ananias and Sapphira commit? Acts 5: 1, 2.

6. How were they punished for this sin?   Acts 5: 1-11.

7. After this, who imprisoned the apostles?   Acts 5:
17, 18.

8. How did they get out of prison?   Acts 5: 19.

9. What did the angel tell them to do?   Acts 5: 20.

10. What did the high priests and others do next morning?   Acts 5: 21-24.

11. When they learned the apostles were in the temple,
what did they do?   Acts 5: 25, 26.

12. Give an account of the trial that followed.   Acts 5:
27-32.

13. Who made a speech in behalf of the apostles?   Acts
5: 34.

14. Give the substance of Gamaliel's speech.   Acts 5: 35-39.

15. What effect did this speech have?   Acts 5: 40.

16. Who brought charges against Stephen?   Acts 6: 8-15.

17. Give the substance of Stephen's speech.   Acts 7: 1-53.

18. How was Stephen treated after making this speech?
Acts 7: 54-60.

19. What prominent character is first mentioned in connection with the stoning of Stephen?   Acts 7: 58.

(Lesson 40—Church Extended by Scattered Disciples)

1. Why were the disciples scattered from Jerusalem?   Acts
8: 1.

2. Who made havoc of the churuch at Jerusalem?   Acts
8: 3.

3. What did these disciples do as they went everywhere?
Acts 8: 4.

4. Who went down to Samaria and preached Christ?   Acts
8: 5.

5. What did the Samaritans do when they believed?   Acts
8: 12.

6. Why did Peter and John go down to Samaria at this
time?   Acts 8: 14-16.

7. How did Peter and John impart the Spirit to the Samaritans?   Acts 8: 17.

8. What man had deceived the Samaritans for a long time?
Acts 8: 9-11.

9. What effect did Philip's preaching have on him? Acts 8: 13.

10. What sin did Simon afterwards commit? Acts 8: 18.

11. How did Peter reprove Simon? Acts 8: 20-22.

12. After this, where did Peter and John go? Acts 8: 25.

13. Where did Philip go from Samaria? Acts 8: 26.

14. What nobleman did Philip convert on his journey? Acts 8: 26-39.

15. What did Philip preach to the eunuch? Acts 8: 35.

16. Give an account of the eunuch's baptism. Acts 8: 36-39.

17. What became of Philip and the eunuch after this? Acts 8: 39.

18. From whom did Paul secure authority to bind Christians? Acts 9: 1, 2.

19. What happened to Saul on his way to Damascus? Acts 9: 3-5.

20. Did those who journeyed with Saul hear and understand what Jesus said to him? Acts 9: 7; 22: 9; 26: 14.

21. Why did Jesus appear to Saul? Acts 26: 16-19.

22. What did Jesus tell Saul to do? Acts 9: 6.

23. Who was sent to tell Saul what to do? Acts 9: 10, 11.

24. How did Ananias feel toward Saul? Acts 9: 13. 14.

25. What did Ananias tell Saul to do? Acts 9: 10, 11; 22: 16.

26. What did Saul do immediately after his baptism? Acts 9: 20.

27. Where did Saul go after this? Gal. 1: 17.

28. When the Jews sought to kill Saul, how did he escape from Damascus? Acts 9: 25.

29. How long after Saul's conversion before he went to Jerusalem? Gal. 1: 11-18.

(Lesson 41—Church Extended by Scattered Disciples—Continued)

1. Where did Saul learn what to preach? Gal. 1: 11, 12.

2. What trouble did Saul have when he reached Jerusalem? Acts 9: 26.

3. Who then introduced him to the disciples? Acts 9: 27.

4. When the Grecians sought to kill him, where did he go? Acts 9: 29, 30.

5. What woman did Peter restore to life at Joppa? Acts 9: 36-42.

6. Mention the good characteristics of Cornelius. Acts 10: 1-4.

7. What did Cornelius see in a vision? Acts 10: 3.

8. What did the angel tell him to do? Acts 10: 4-6.

9. Who went to Joppa after Peter? Acts 10: 7.

10. What vision did Peter have just before the messengers reached him? Acts 10: 9-17.

11. What was this vision intended to teach Peter? Acts 10: 28.

12. What did Peter preach to Cornelius? Acts 10: 34-43.

13. What occurred as Peter was speaking? Acts 10: 44.

14. What amazed the Jews who came with Peter? Acts 10: 45.

15. How did they know the Gentiles had received the Spirit? Acts 10: 46.

16. What was the purpose of the baptism of the Holy Spirit? Acts 11: 15-18.

17. What did Peter then command? Acts 10: 46, 47.

18. What trouble did Peter have about this when he went back to Jerusalem? Acts 11: 2.

19. How did Peter defend himself? Acts 11: 4-18.

20. Who started the work in Antioch? Acts 11: 19-21.

21. Who came to Antioch on hearing of the "big meeting?" Acts 11: 22-24.

22. Where did Barnabas next go, and why? Acts 11: 25.

23. How long did this meeting continue after Saul came to Antioch? Acts 11: 25, 26.

24. What name did the disciples now receive for the first time? Acts 11: 26.

25. How did the Antioch church manifest interest in the brethren in Judea? Acts 11: 27-30.

26. Which one of the apostles did Herod kill? Acts 12: 1, 2.

27. What other apostle did he purpose to kill, and why did he fail? Acts 12: 3-19.

28. Give an account of Herod's death.   Acts 12: 20-23.

29. Who came with Barnabas and Saul back from Jerusalem?   Acts 12: 25.

(Lesson 42—Paul's First Missionary Journey)

1. Under what circumstances were Barnabas and Saul sent out as missionaries?   Acts 13: 1-3.

2. Who accompanied them on this journey?   Acts 13: 5.

3. From what seaport did they sail?   Acts 13: 4.

4. To what island did they sail?   Acts 13: 4.

5. Mention two places visited on this island.   Acts 13: 5, 6.

6. What miracle was performed at Paphos?   Acts 13: 6-12.

7. Who was converted at Paphos?   Acts 13: 6-12.

8. After leaving Cyprus, where did they next stop?   Acts 13: 13.

9. What do you know about John Mark at this time?   Acts 13: 13.

10. After leaving Perga, what was the next stop?   Acts 13: 14.

11. Where did Paul address the people of Antioch?   Acts 13: 14-16.

12. Give the substance of Paul's sermon to the people of Antioch.   Acts 13: 16-41.

13. What request did they make of Paul after this sermon?   Acts 13: 42.

14. What do you know about the audience that greeted Paul the next Sabbath?   Acts 13: 44.

15. How did this affect the Jews, and what did they do?   Acts 13: 45-50.

16. After this, where did Paul and Barnabas go?   Acts 13: 51.

17. Give an account of their stay at Iconium.   Acts 14: 1-5.

18. Where did they go from Iconium?   Acts 14: 6, 7.

19. At what place did the people attempt to sacrifice to Paul?   Acts 14: 11-18.

20. Why were they disposed to look upon Paul as a god?   Acts 14: 8-12.

21. Later, how was Paul treated at Lystra?   Acts 14: 19.

22. To what place did they go after leaving Lystra? Acts 14: 20.

23. What places did they revisit on their homeward journey? Acts 14: 21-25.

24. Why did they revisit these cities? Acts 14: 21-25.

25. When they reached Antioch (in Syria), what did they do? Acts 14: 26, 27.

(Lesson 43—The Question of Circumcision)

1. What trouble arose in the Antioch church about this time? Acts 15: 1.

2. How did the brethren decide to settle the question? Acts 15: 2.

3. What places did Paul and Barnabas visit on the way to Jerusalem? Acts 15: 3.

4. What message did they deliver as they passed along? Acts 15: 3.

5. When they reached Jerusalem, before whom did they go? Acts 15: 4.

6. Who contended for circumcising the Gentiles in this meeting? Acts 15: 5.

7. Who then made a speech to the apostles and elders? Acts 15: 7.

8. Give the substance of Peter's address. Acts 15: 7-10.

9. Who next made a speech on the subject? Acts 15: 13.

10. Give the substance of James' speech. Acts 15: 13-21.

11. Who was then selected to go with Paul and Barnabas back to Antioch? Acts 15: 22.

12. Give the substance of the apostles and elders' letter to the church at Antioch. Acts 15: 23-29.

13. How was this letter received at Antioch? Acts 15: 30.

14. In addition to delivering the letter, what did Judas and Silas do? Acts 15: 32.

15. After they had spent some time there, what did the brethren do? Acts 15: 33.

16. Immediately following this, what did Paul and Barnabas do? Acts 15: 33.

17. After this, what proposition did Paul make to Barnabas? Acts 15: 36.

18. Why did Paul and Barnabas separate at this time?
Acts 15: 37-39.

19. What became of Barnabas and John Mark?   Acts
15: 39.

20. Do we have any further record of Barnabas' work?
No.

21. What reference does Paul make to Barnabas after this?
1 Cor. 9: 6; Gal. 2: 9, 13.

22. What reference does Paul afterwards make to Mark?
Col. 4: 10; 2 Tim. 4: 11.

23. Whom did Paul choose as his traveling companion?
Acts 15: 40.

(Lesson 44—Paul's Second Missionary Journey)

1. What route did Paul and Silas take on this journey?
Acts 15: 41.

2. What seems to have been the purpose in making this
journey?   Acts 15: 36, 41.

3. At what place did Timothy join Paul and Silas?   Acts
16: 1-3.

4. What did they do as they passed from city to city?
Acts 16: 4.

5. How did their visits affect the churches?   Acts 16: 5.

6. What provinces in Asia Minor did they pass through?
Acts 16: 6-9.

7. Why did they not continue to preach in Asia?   Acts
16: 6.

8. What vision did Paul have at Troas?   Acts 16: 8, 9.

9. Who seems to have joined Paul's company at Troas?
Acts 16: 10.

10. From Troas to what island did they sail?   Acts 16: 11.

11. What was the next step?   Acts 16: 11.

12. Where did they go from Neapolis?   Acts 16: 16.

13. What do you know about the city of Philippi?   Acts
16: 12.

14. What did Paul and his company do on the Sabbath
day?   Acts 16: 13.

15. What woman was converted at this time?   Acts 16: 14.

16. How did she show her appreciation for what they did
for her?   Acts 16: 15.

17. What miracle did Paul perform on a certain maid? Acts 16: 16-18.

18. Why were her masters offended? Acts 16: 16-19.

19. How were Paul and Silas then treated? Acts 16: 19-24.

(Lesson 45—Paul's Second Missionary Journey —Continued)

1. How did God interfere in behalf of Paul and Silas? Acts 16: 25, 26.

2. Give an account of the jailer's conversion. Acts 16: 27-34.

3. What word did the magistrates send the jailer next morning? Acts 16: 35, 36.

4. What answer did Paul make to this? Acts 16: 37.

5. When the magistrates heard what Paul said, what did they do? Acts 16: 38, 39.

6. Where did they go before leaving the city, and why? Acts 16: 40.

7. Who seems to have been left at Philippi? Acts 16: 17-40.

8. Where did Paul and his company go from Philippi? Acts 17: 1.

9. Where did Paul preach in Thessalonica? Acts 17: 1, 2.

10. How long did he remain in Thessalonica? Acts 17: 2; Phil. 4: 15, 16.

11. What was the burden of Paul's preaching? Acts 17: 3.

12. What was the result of his labor at this time? Acts 17: 4.

13. With whom did Paul and Silas lodge at Thessalonica? Acts 17: 5-9.

14. How was Jason treated for entertaining them? Acts 17: 5-9.

15. After this, where did the brethren send Paul and Silas? Acts 17: 10.

16. How did the historian (Luke) contrast the people of Thessalonica and those of Berea? Acts 17: 11.

17. What was the result of Paul's preaching at Berea? Acts 17: 12.

18. Who stirred up the people of Berea against Paul? **Acts** 17: 13.

19. Where did Paul go from Berea?   Acts 17: 14, 15.

(Lesson 46—Paul's Second Missionary Journey— Continued)

1. Who were left at Berea?   Acts 17: 14.

2. What did Paul do in Athens while waiting for Silas and Timothy?   Acts 17: 16, 17.

3. What did the philosophers think of Paul?   Acts 17: 18-20.

4. From what place did Paul address the Athenians? Acts 17: 22.

5. Give the substance of Paul's speech.   Acts 17: 22-31.

6. What was the result of this preaching?   Acts 17: 32-34.

7. From Athens where did Paul go?   Acts 18: 1.

8. With whom did Paul stop at Corinth?   Acts 18: 2, 3.

9. What did Paul do each Sabbath day?   Acts 18: 4.

10. Who rejoined Paul at Corinth?   Acts 18: 5.

11. Why did Paul turn to the Gentiles at this time?   Acts 18: 6.

12. In whose house did Paul now preach?   Acts 18: 7.

13. What is said of the results of Paul's preaching here? Acts 18: 8.

14. How was Paul encouraged at this time?   Acts 18: 9, 10.

15. What experience did Paul have before Gallio?   Acts 18: 12-16.

16. How was Sosthenes treated at this time?   Acts 18: 17.

17. How long did Paul preach at Corinth?   Acts 18: 11-18.

18. On leaving Corinth, who went with Paul?   Acts 18: 18.

19. Where did they go from Corinth?   Acts 18: 19.

20. Who was left at Ephesus?   Acts 18: 19.

21. Where did Paul go from Ephesus?   Acts 18: 20-22.

(Lesson 47—Paul's Third Missionary Journey)

1. Mention two provinces in Asia Minor visited by Paul on this journey. Acts 18: 23.

2. What was Paul's object in visiting the disciples in these regions? Acts 18: 23.

3. At what place did Paul spend more than two years? Acts 19: 1-10.

4. As a result of Paul's stay at Ephesus who heard the word? Acts 19: 10.

5. Where did Paul preach for the first three months in Ephesus? Acts 19: 8.

6. Why did he leave the synagogue, and where did he go? Acts 19: 9.

7. What special miracles did God work through Paul? Acts 19: 11, 12.

8. What do you know about the seven sons of Sceva? Acts 18: 13-16.

9. What effect did this have on the people of Ephesus? Acts 19: 17-20.

10. What was the price of the books they burned at this time? Acts 19: 19.

11. What two disciples did Paul send from Ephesus to Macedonia? Acts 19: 22.

12. Who was Demetrius, and how did he instigate a riot? Acts 19: 23-28.

13. Describe the temple of Diana. See Bible dictionary.

14. How long did the mob cry, " Great is Diana of the Ephesians? " Acts 19: 34.

15. What did the Ephesians think about the image of Diana? Acts 19: 35.

16. Who quieted and dismissed the mob? Acts 19: 35-41.

17. Where did Paul go from Ephesus? Acts 20: 1.

(Lesson 48—Paul's Third Missionary Journey— Continued)

1. What was Paul's mission in Macedonia, and from there where did he go? Acts 20: 2.

2. How long did he remain in Greece? Acts 20: 3.

3. Why did he return by the way of Macedonia? **Acts** 20: 3.

4. What city did he visit in Macedonia? Acts 20: 6.

5. Mention Paul's companions at this time. Acts 20: 4-6.

6. From Philippi where did they go? Acts 20: 6.

7. How long did they stay at Troas? Acts 20: 6.

8. What did they do on the first day of the week? **Acts** 20: 7.

9. What miracle did Paul perform at that time? Acts 20: 8-12.

10. Mention three places on the route from Troas to Miletus. Acts 20: 13-15.

11. Whom did Paul send for from Miletus? Acts 20: 17.

12. Give the substance of Paul's speech to these elders. Acts 20: 18-35.

13. Why did these elders sorrow so on Paul's leaving them? Acts 20: 36-38.

14. Where did Paul land in Syria this time? Acts 21: 1-3.

15. Mention two places on the route from Miletus to Tyre. Acts 21: 1-3.

16. How long did they remain in Tyre? Acts 21: 4.

17. How did the disciples at Tyre show appreciation of Paul? Acts 21: 5, 6.

18. At what place did Paul spend a day on his way from Tyre to Cesarea? Acts 21: 7, 8.

19. What noted evangelist did Paul visit at Cesarea? Acts 21: 8.

20. What prophet came down from Jerusalem to see Paul? Acts 21: 10.

21. What did Agabus prophesy concerning Paul? Acts 21: 11.

22. What answer did Paul make when the disciples pleaded with him not to go up to Jerusalem? Acts 21: 12-14.

23. From Cesarea where did Paul go? Acts 21: 15.

(Lesson 49—Paul Apprehended at Jerusalem)

1. At the close of Paul's third missionary journey who went with him up to Jerusalem? Acts 21: 16.

2. Mention the different times Paul had been in Jerusa-

lem since his conversion.   Acts 9 : 26; 12 : 25; 15 : 1-6; 18 : 22; 21 : 15.

3. How was Paul received by the brethren on his last visit?   Acts 21 : 17.

4. What advice did James and others give Paul at this time?   Acts 21 : 17-26.

5. Who stirred up the multitude against Paul?   Acts 21 : 27.

6. What charges did they bring against Paul?   Acts 21 : 28.

7. Were these charges true?   Acts 21 : 29; 24 : 11-13.

8. How was Paul further treated at this time?   Acts 21 : 30, 31.

9. Who rescued Paul from the mob?   Acts 21 : 32.

10. What did they do with him?   Acts 21 : 33-36.

11. What request did Paul make of the chief captain?   Acts 21 : 37-40.

12. Give the substance of Paul's speech at this time.   Acts 22 : 1-20.

13. How was his speech interrupted?   Acts 22 : 21-24.

14. What did the captain then purpose to do?   Acts 22 : 24.

15. How did Paul defend himself in this matter?   Acts 22 : 25-29.

16. On the next day what was done with Paul?   Acts 22 : 30.

17. Give an account of this examination.   Acts 23 : 1-10.

18. How was Paul encouraged the following night?   Acts 23 : 11.

19. What wicked plot was laid at this time to kill Paul?   Acts 23 : 12-15.

20. How was this plot made known to the captain?   Acts 23 : 16-22.

21. What did the captain then do with Paul?   Acts 23 : 23, 24.

22. Give the substance of the captain's letter to Felix.   Acts 23 : 25-30.

23. Where was Paul kept as a prisoner in Cesarea?   Acts 23 : 31-35.

(Lesson 50—Paul's Experience at Cesarea)

1. Where did our last lesson leave Paul? Acts 23: 31-35.

2. Who came down from Jerusalem to accuse Paul? Acts 24: 1.

3. How did Tertullus introduce his speech before Felix? Acts 24: 2-4.

4. What charges did Tertullus bring against Paul? Acts 24: 5-9.

5. Give the substance of Paul's speech in defense of himself. Acts 24: 10-21.

6. How did this trial terminate? Acts 24: 22.

7. How was Paul treated as a prisoner in Cesarea? Acts 24: 23.

8. Give an account of the next meeting Felix had with Paul. Acts 24: 25.

9. Why did Felix frequently send for Paul? Acts 24: 26.

10. Why was Paul left a prisoner when Felix was succeeded by Festus? Acts 24: 27.

11. How long had Paul been a prisoner at Cesarea? Acts 24: 27.

12. How did the Jews at Jerusalem at this time attempt to have Paul killed? Acts 25: 1-3.

13. What did Festus answer to their resquest? Acts 25: 4, 5.

14. What about the charges these Jews brought against Paul at this time? Acts 25: 7.

15. To these charges what did Paul answer? Acts 25: 8.

16. Why did Paul appeal to Cæsar? Acts 25: 9-12.

17. Give Festus' rehearsal of the case before Agrippa. Acts 25: 13-21.

18. Then what request did Agrippa make? Acts 25: 22.

19. How was Paul introduced to Agrippa and the company the next day? Acts 25: 23-27.

20. Give the substance of Paul's speech before Agrippa. Acts 26: 2-23.

21. How did this speech affect Festus? Acts 26: 24.

22. How did Paul answer Festus? Acts 26: 25, 26.

23 Then what question did Paul put direct to Agrippa? Acts 26: 27.

24. What answer did Agrippa make?   Acts 26: 28.

25. What reply did Paul make to this?   Acts 26: 29.

26. What was the decision of all who heard Paul that day? Acts 26: 30, 31.

27. What did Agrippa say to Festus after they retired? Acts 26: 32.

(Lesson 51—Paul's Voyage to Rome)

1. Who had charge of Paul on the voyage to Rome? Acts 27: 1.

2. What disciple was with Paul on the voyage?   Acts 27: 1, 2.

3. From Cesarea where did they go?   Acts 27: 3.

4. What privilege did Paul enjoy at Sidon?   Acts 27: 3.

5. Where did they next land, and by what island did they pass?   Aets 27: 4, 5.

6. What change was made at Myra?   Acts 27: 6.

7. From Myra where did they go?   Acts 27: 7, 8.

8. What advice did Paul offer before leaving Fair Havens?   Acts 27: 9, 10, 21.

9. How was Paul's advice treated?   Acts 27: 11.

10. Why did they not wish to spend the winter in Fair Havens, and where did they hope to spend the winter?   Acts 27: 12.

11. Why did they not go to Phenice?   Acts 27: 13-15.

12. What does the word "Euroclydon" ("Euraquilo" in Revised Version) mean?   See Bible dictionary.

13. What small island did they pass soon after leaving Crete?   Acts 27: 16.

14. What did they do as a precaution at Clauda?   Acts 27: 16, 17.

15. On the next day, and the third day, what did they do further?   Acts 27: 18, 19.

16. How did the whole company now feel as to their safety? Acts 27: 20.

17. At this time how did Paul comfort them?   Acts 27: 21-26.

18. How long were they driven before the breath of the storm?   Acts 27: 27-33.

19. How many were on this vessel?   Acts 27: 37.

20. Give an account of the shipwreck. Acts 27: 38-41.

21. What did the sailors purpose to do, and how were they hindered? Acts 27: 42, 43.

22. Give an account of their landing. Acts 27: 43, 44.

23. On what island did they land? Acts 28: 1.

24. How did the people of the island treat them? Acts 28: 2.

25. Why did these superstitious people think Paul was a god? Acts 28: 3-6.

26. What miracles did Paul perform on this island? Acts 28: 7-9.

27. How long did they remain on the island of Melita? Acts 28: 11.

28. After leaving Melita, where did they next stop, and how long did they stay? Acts 28: 12.

29. What was the next stop, and how long did they stay? Acts 28: 13.

30. At what place did they land in Italy? Acts 28: 13.

31. How long did Paul and his company remain at Puteoli, and why? Acts 28: 14.

32. Where did the brethren from Rome meet Paul? Acts 28: 15.

33. How was Paul treated when he reached Rome? Acts 28: 16.

34. Give the substance of Paul's address to the chief Jews. Acts 28: 17-20.

35. What answer did these chief Jews make to Paul? Acts 28: 21, 22.

36. Give the substance of Paul's address to the great company later on. Acts 28: 23-28.

37. How long did Paul remain in Rome, and where? Acts 28: 30.

38. What did Paul do all this time? Acts 28: 31.

39. What further do you know about Paul? It is generally believed that he was acquitted by Nero after about two years' imprisonment, and that he made another tour of the churches, and, after this, was imprisoned the second time at Rome, where he perished in the great persecution of Christians by Nero in the year 66 or 67 A.D

(Lesson 52—General Questions)

(For answers to these questions let the student draw on the stock of information gathered in passing through the Bible. Where he fails to recall the answer, diligent search should be made until the answer is discovered. This will be found an interesting and profitable lesson.)

1. Locate the Holy Land.
2. Mention four names by which it is called.
3. In the broadest sense, what does Palestine include?
4. Name and locate the three divisions of Palestine.
5. What does the expression, "from Dan to Beersheba," literally mean?
6. Name and locate three important Bible rivers.
7. Mention one event connected with each of these rivers.
8. What river ran through the city of Babylon?
9. Mention one peculiarity of the Nile River.
10. Name and locate three important Bible seas.
11. Mention one event connected with each of these seas.
12. On and near what sea did Jesus perform most of his miracles?
13. Mention one peculiarity of the Dead Sea.
14. Name and locate three Bible mountains.
15. Mention one event connected with each of these mountains.
16. On what mountain did Moses receive the law?
17. On what mountain did Aaron die?
18. From what mountain did Moses view the promised land?
19. On what mountain did the temple stand?
20. On what mountain was Jesus transfigured?
21. From what mountain did Jesus ascend?
22. On what mountain did Abraham prepare to offer Isaac?
23. What great battle was fought near Mount Tabor?
24. Name and locate three islands mentioned in the Bible.
25. Mention one event connected with each of these islands.
26. Name three Bible cities that begin with "A."
27. Mention one event connected with each of these cities.
28. Name three Bible cities that begin with " B."
29. Mention one event connected with each of these cities.
30. Name three Bible cities that begin with " C."

31. Mention one event connected with each of these cities.
32. Name two Bible cities that begin with " D."
33. Mention one event connected with each of these cities.
34. Mention one important Bible city that begins with " E."
35. Name two Bible cities that begin with " G."
36. Mention one event connected with each of these cities.
37. Name two Bible cities that begin with " H."
38. Mention one event connected with each of these cities.
39. Name three Bible cities that begin with "J."
40. Mention one event connected with each of these cities.
41. Name and locate one Bible city that begins with " M."
42. Name two Bible cities that begin with " N."
43. Mention one event connected with each of these cities.
44. Name and locate one Bible city that begins with " P."
45. Name and locate one Bible city that begins with " R."
46. Name three Bible cities that begin with " S."
47. Mention one event connected with each of these cities.
48. Name three Bible cities that begin with " T."
49. Mention one event connected with each of these cities.
50. Name and locate one Bible city that begins with " U."

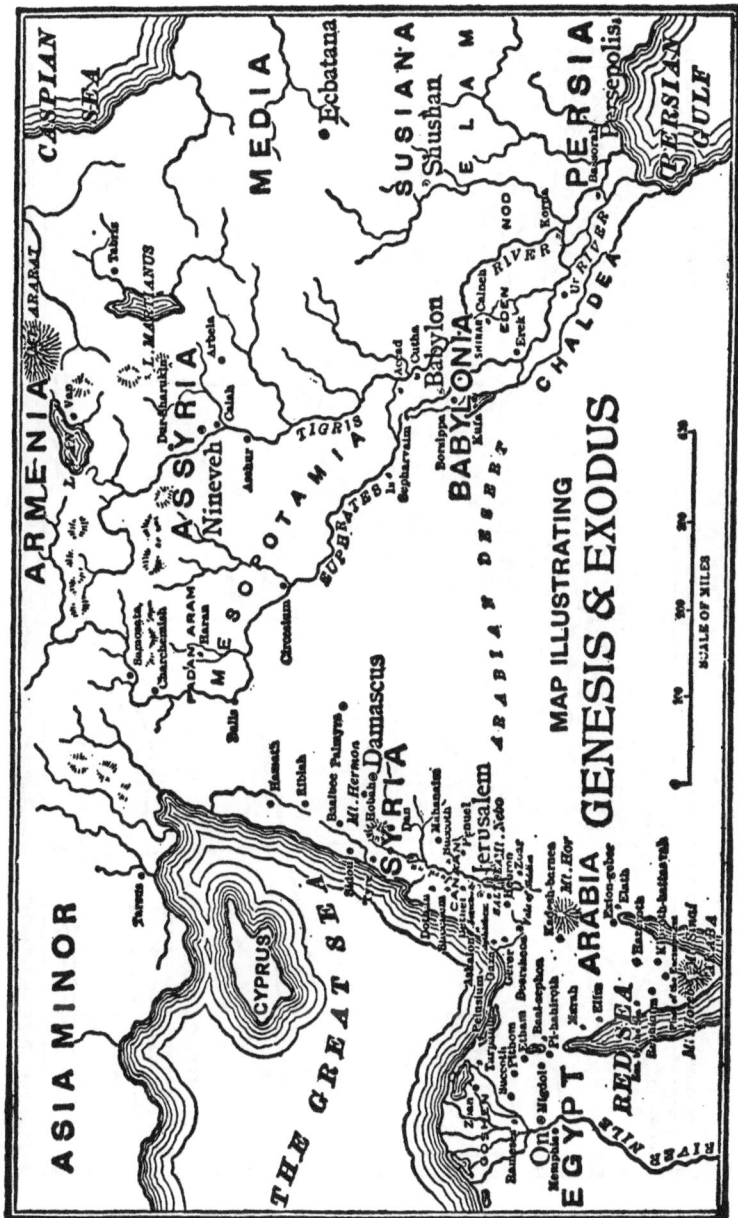

MAP ILLUSTRATING

GENESIS & EXODUS

SCALE OF MILES

ASIA MINOR

ARMENIA

ARARAT

CASPIAN SEA

MEDIA

Tabriz

Ecbatana

SUSIANA

Shushan

ELAM

PERSIA

Persepolis

PERSIAN GULF

L. Van

ASSYRIA

Dur-Sharukin

Nineveh

Calah

Arbela

TIGRIS

MESOPOTAMIA

EUPHRATES

Sippara

Agad

Cutha

Babylon

BABYLONIA

Borsippa

Kutha

EDEN

Erech

NOD

RIVER

CHALDEA

DAMARAM

Haran

Charchamish

Circesium

Palmyra

SYRIA

Damascus

Baalbec

Mt. Hermon

Dan

Jerusalem

CANAAN

Mt. Nebo

ARABIAN DESERT

Hamath

Riblah

Kadesh-barnea

Mt. Hor

Ezion-geber

ARABIA

CYPRUS

THE GREAT SEA

Elim

EGYPT

On

Memphis

Pithom

RED SEA

RIVER NILE

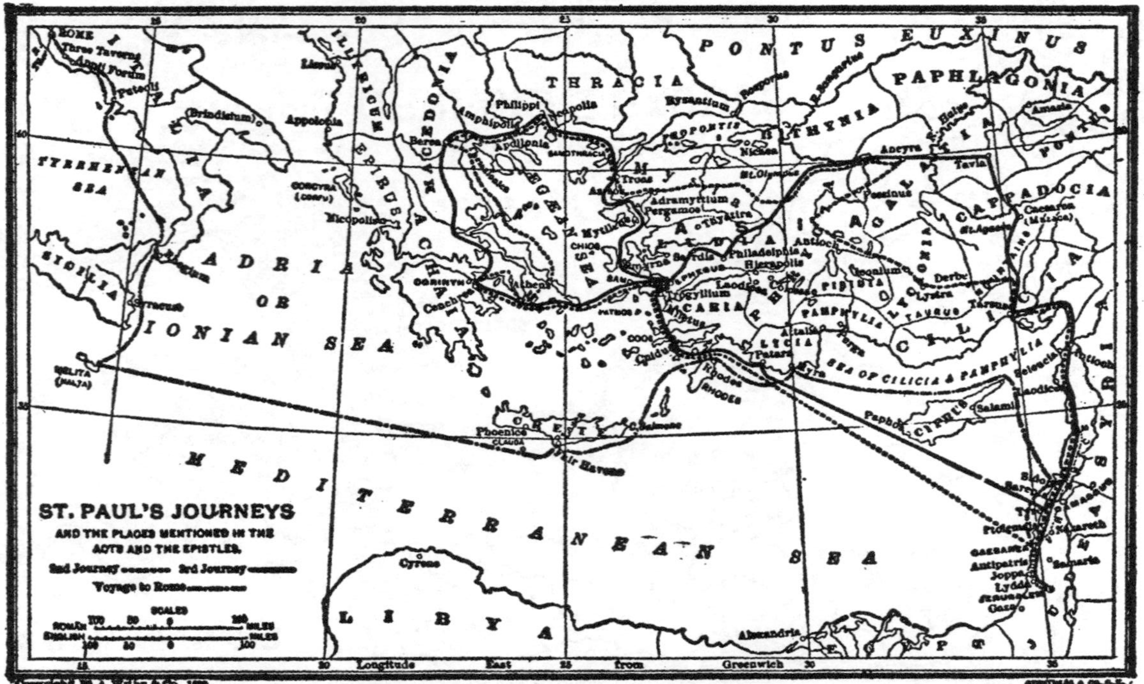

ST. PAUL'S JOURNEYS
AND THE PLACES MENTIONED IN THE ACTS AND THE EPISTLES.
2nd Journey
3rd Journey
Voyage to Rome
SCALES
ROMAN
ENGLISH
MILES
Longitude
East
from
Greenwich
PONTUS EUXINUS
PAPHLAGONIA
THRACIA
MACEDONIA
ILLYRICUM
EPIRUS
ACHAIA
BITHYNIA
CAPPADOCIA
CILICIA
PISIDIA
PAMPHYLIA
LYCIA
CARIA
CYPRUS
SYRIA
LIBYA
EGYPT
ADRIA OR IONIAN SEA
MEDITERRANEAN SEA
SEA OF CILICIA & PAMPHYLIA
TYRRHENIAN SEA
SICILIA
AEGEAN SEA
ROME
Three Taverns
Appii Forum
Puteoli
(Brindisium)
Appolonia
Nicopolis
CORCYRA (CORFU)
MELITA (MALTA)
Syracuse
Berea
Amphipolis
Philippi
Neapolis
Apollonia
SAMOTHRACIA
Byzantium
Bosporus
PROPONTIS
Nicaea
Troas
Assos
Adramyttium
Pergamos
Thyatira
Mytilene
CHIOS
Smyrna
Sardis
Philadelphia
Hierapolis
Laodicea
Colosse
Antioch
Iconium
Lystra
Derbe
Tarsus
TAURUS
Ancyra
Tavia
Pessinus
St. Olympus
Caesarea (Mazaca)
Amasia
Corinth
Cenchrea
Athens
PATMOS
Trogyllium
Miletus
COOS
Cnidus
Rhodes
RHODES
Patara
Myra
Attalia
Perga
Seleucia
Antioch
Laodicea
Salamis
Paphos
Phoenice
CLAUDA
Fair Havens
C. Salmone
Sidon
Sarepta
Tyre
Ptolemais
Nazareth
Caesarea
Antipatris
Samaria
Joppa
Lydda
Jerusalem
Gaza
Cyrene
Alexandria

MAP OF
PALESTINE
IN THE TIME OF OUR
SAVIOUR

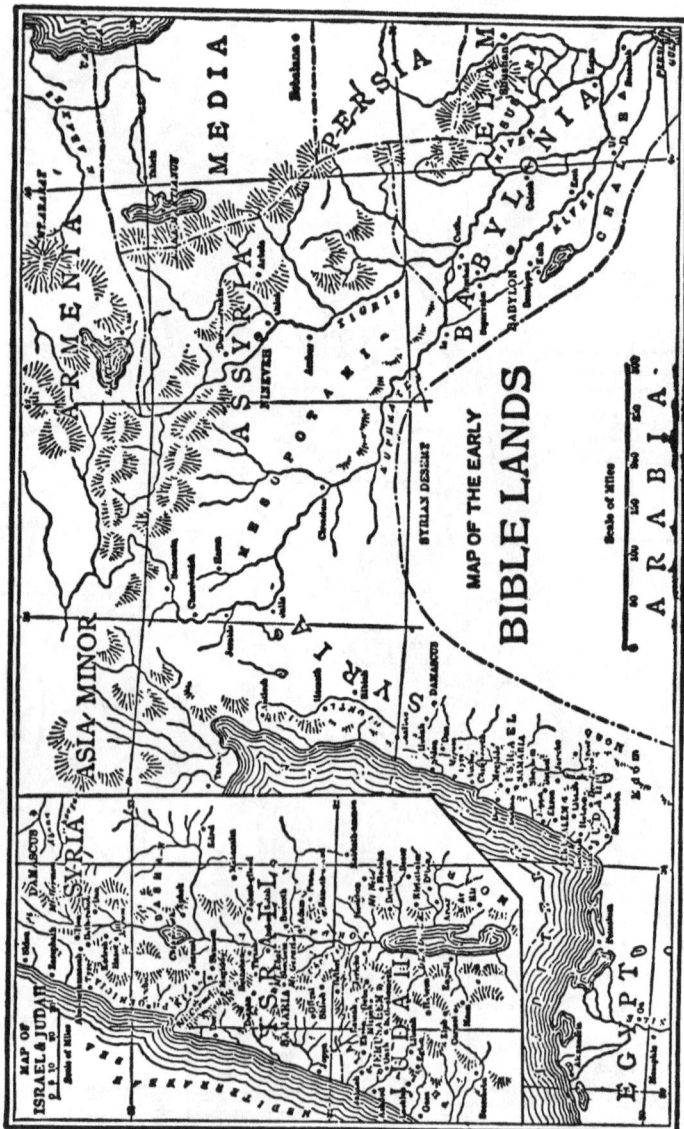

MAP OF THE EARLY
BIBLE LANDS

Scale of Miles

MAP OF
ISRAEL & JUDAH

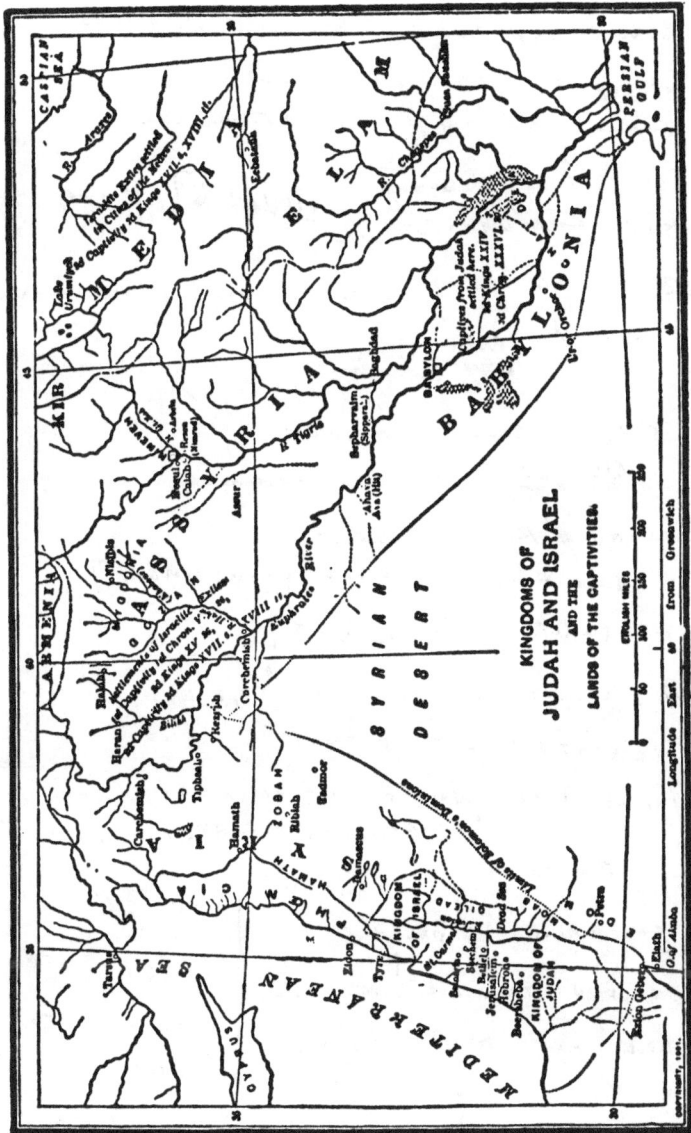

KINGDOMS OF
JUDAH AND ISRAEL
AND THE
LANDS OF THE CAPTIVITIES

"FATHERS" 6/16/24
                    ANDY G. V HOMERS:
D. ROLE HAS BEEN DIMINISHED
                    • DIFF. BTWN TWO ∧∧.
D. OUR FATHER ∧.IN HEAVEN ∧. ←HE IDETTFYS?
STATS: 63-% (FATHERLESS HOMES)
fatherless GEN.   80% RADTST   70% H.S. DROPOUTS
  2x LIKLY TO DROP OUT   75% - CHEM. ABUSE
——: MAN/WOMAN   MARRY. GEZ →FOLLOWTNG.

GOD HAS EST. A PATTERN. I
KARATE KID: father: teach   [DUET 6] V. 1-9 +
V. 20 (V. 2 FEAR THE LORD.) (OBSERVE/OBEY) (EMPH. ✓ LOVE GOD)
[TEACH THEM DTLGH.] father teach

①. WISDOM HAS NOT BEEN PASSED DOWN.
EPN 6.4   COL 3.21 ——→ NOT OVERBEARING.

II. DISCIPLINE & RESPONSIBILTY
  ∆ NEED TO HAVE THAT DISCIPLINE [CHASTISMENT.]
REV 3.19 (TELL A FAULT)   HEB. 12. 5-7 ✓
PROV. 3. 11-12 (HE LOVES, HE CORRECTS)   13. 24
  ↓
22:15   UNTRAINED /UNDISCIPLINED
(MEN: DANGEROUS) ∆∆ [NOT MATTER OF ANGER/WRATH:]
                    CORRECTING MISBEHAVIOR
LLL LOVE + BLESS

D. PROVEDE for them   ∆. BALANCE |ADVICE
                          ↑ |•ENJOY THEM
∆. GREAT MEN, OFTEN: TERRIBLE CHILDREN |
                                        |• LALL BACK TO
∆. BE A SIMPLE MAN; ∆. BE THERE | DUET.
                                        |+ LOVE THEM /
• PROV 13. 1 | LOVE HIM.